B.LITTLE

What Doesn't Kill You Makes a Good Story
A "How-NOT-To" Guide to College

Brittney Ann Little

This book is dedicated to my parents. Without you two, I would have never gotten into college, I would have never graduated college, and I would have never had the courage or tools necessary to write this book. Thank you for filling our house with literature, laughter, and most importantly, country music. I love you.

Prologue/Disclaimer:

Getting into college was the easy part. It really was. I had gotten into all six of the schools that I had applied to (3 in the Big Ten, 1 Illinois state school, and 2 private schools...although I am not bragging...), but I had never thought that making it to graduation was going to be this difficult.

Everything you are about to read happened to me. I don't have superpowers, I am not a vampire nor about to be one (nor do I want to be, in case you were wondering). I am not magical in any way, shape, or form. I am just a survivor and a dreamer. I'm a regular girl hailing from the Chicago suburbs. I have great parents, a wonderful brother, and amazing friends. I drive a beat-up 2001 Ford Explorer. I shop at Target and Forever 21. Essentially, I am the dictionary definition of a normal suburban girl (minus the white picket fence...I mean, our house has a white fence...but it's not a picket fence – apparently there is a difference).

This is what happened according to ME and from MY perspective. This is the story of my (slightly humorous and thickly sarcastic) journey through the roughest four years I ever loved at Indiana University in Bloomington, Indiana.

These are the big adventures of me, Brittney Ann Little. These are all the things you WISH you knew about college. It may be pretentious to say but...you're welcome.

Prelude to Terror: Freshman Year

It started with a haircut.

Actually, it probably started with my conception and/or birth and the genes and millions of molecules that came together to create the magical creature that is me.

But if I had to pick another moment that began my utter hell, it was definitely this haircut.

For some reason, a large majority of females who are high school seniors feel the need to chop their hair off in the hopes that it makes them all "different" and "grown up" for college.

Unfortunately, I was no exception.

Lesson Number 1: A haircut will NOT change your life.

As long as I could remember, I had had long, blond hair. In fact, my mother would not let me get a legitimate salon hair cut until I was in seventh grade. She herself trimmed an inch off every few months. My hair's immaculate length remained my signature throughout my Catholic high school years and it was about to be chopped off.

How was I supposed to know that all of my power and strength were wrapped up in that hair? I was a female Samson. The second that hair hit the floor, I was done for.

But of course, I did not know that. In fact, I cheerily walked into the salon with a few photos of short-haired girls, sat down, and told my stylist that it was what I wanted. When it was over, I paid her, walked out, and sent photos of my new look to my best friend Lizzie. At the time, I thought this had been a great idea. At the time, I thought a lot of things were a great idea.

In a reassuring way, Lizzie finally texted back, "Oh my gosh Bee I love it!" after receiving what is best described as a million pictures from different angles of the new 'do. Lizzie calls me "Bee" which is short for Brittney. While Brittney is not a long name to say, I hate being called "Britt" and much prefer Lizzie's version of my nickname. Lizzie and I met doing the Joffrey Ballet of Chicago's Nutcracker and instantly bonded over the fact that we were a) the same height, b) looked a lot alike, and c) very miscast as "serene and gentle" angels in the production. Lizzie and I are two peas in a pod. We are the epitome of energetic and are quite entertaining when we get together. She's been my best friend since sixth grade, and is definitely my consult for hair and beauty advice. Everyone should have a friend like that. In fact, some people should have two.

So, I went forth to college, soothed by my hair expert's opinion on my new cut. As many college freshmen do, I dreamt of a new beginning and of new and exciting experiences. I guess you could say my drive to Bloomington, Indiana was comparable to a video montage with a matching soundtrack very similar to the beginning of pretty much every chick flick or Disney Channel movie that you have ever seen. Looking back, the song would be "Good Girl" by Carrie Underwood, with images painted in clouds. There would be me going to football games on the arm of some frat boy cutie, me making best friends with the most popular girls on campus, and me studying under a tree in the quad all seamlessly transforming into one another along with Carrie crooning in the background. That was what my drive down to Bloomington was, just a giant montage of high hopes and unrealistic expectations.

Lesson Number 2: No Expectations = No Disappointments.

Here was the problem: I seriously had no idea why I was going to college. It seemed like the next logical step to take, but I really had no grand plans to get a degree. To me, college seemed like a sick experiment. Think about it: you take 40,000 or more 18- to 22-year-olds and stick them in a small town with liquor and homework to help them pass the time. What do YOU think is going to happen?

I had always planned to be a musician, a dream that I would not attain with my degree. But music was not a rational career choice, and I needed to get a degree in something that would make me money. It was for that reason that I was headed towards college.

I was dead set against college, but I had no way out. I was ~~encouraged~~ forced to give it a shot, to make the most of it. So I found myself on I-65, stuck in the car with my mom, my dad, and a few thousand of my most prized possessions.

Sounds like fun right?

Wrong.

Lesson Number 3: How NOT to make a first impression.

Moving in was a nightmare. Seriously. No wonder my Dad has lived in the same house since he was a kid. The dorm was not air conditioned, so we all climbed up the stairs with box after box to a stuffy room which looked more or less like a prison cell, but with better closet space. To illustrate further the trauma that was "move in day," my outfit was horrendous. I wore my worst pair of flared jeans, a white lace cami layered over a solid red cami, and a XXXL "Illinois State" hoodie stolen from a guy friend was tied around my waist. My "new hair" was in a pile on top of my head, and sweat covered my un-made up face.

Oh yeah. I was really turning heads at Indiana University.

Lesson Number 4: Making friends and living with friends –

good luck with that...

My roommate Maggie and I had known each other since fourth grade, but had never been close friends. Most of her stuff was green, my stuff was pink, and we had a pretty cute room once the parents left. Unfortunately, the parents did have to leave eventually. It wasn't that I wanted my mom and dad to stay. The 9-by-14 room would be crowded with them tagging along for the collegiate ride. It wasn't too hard to watch them go, but the awkward silence in which they left Maggie and I was hard to break.

"So...how's Niko?" I ventured, asking about her long-term, and now long-distance, boyfriend.

"Oh good," Maggie said back.

Clearly, we are both amazing conversationalists.

Luckily, we met Jenny (who lived across the hall) and Hannah (who lived next door), who were both left without a roommate after move-in.

Hannah was from Middletown, Indiana, a small town without a stoplight in sight. She was like a Gilmore Girl come to life...so witty and so quick it made you feel smart just to keep up a conversation with her. The most entertaining part about having Hannah on the floor was how uncomfortable she made some of the ditzy girls on the floor. Hannah can whip out a pop culture reference, watch someone squirm to understand it, and not once try and explain it to them. It's fairly amusing to watch, really.

On the other end of the spectrum is Jenny. Every ounce of that girl oozes innocence and perfection. She was an IU cheerleader, a near-perfect student, and a loyal friend. Jenny was always one step ahead, and one notch above me. We were both blond (although Jenny was blonder) with blue eyes and pale skin (although Jenny's skin was clearer) and we were both short (although Jenny was more athletically built). We got along from the start because in a lot of ways we were similar. I was enthralled by her cheer experience, fascinated in her large makeup selection, and mesmerized by her wardrobe. I knew we would become good friends.

Because the dorm did not have air conditioning, my new hair spent its days in a sticky mess – either hot on my neck or on top of my head. This was doing wonderful things for my self-esteem. My bangs constantly curled in weird ways, my usually straight locks seemed to frizz constantly…

I was a one-woman freak show.

What really and eventually gave me confidence in the haircut was Brendan. He was a male cheerleader/ROTC hottie friend of Jenny's who also happened to be a freshman. He was tall, dark, and oh-so-handsome, with mouthwatering biceps and a genuine smile. I ended up spending my first night out at the free movie at the student union with Jenny, Hannah, Maggie, Brendan, and a few of his friends.

Lesson Number 5: How to meet guys (The Embarrassing Way)

My embarrassing first encounter with a college guy went a little something like this:

Brendan: "Hey, I am Brendan. You kind of remind me of Lo from Laguna Beach."

Me: (nervous laughter)

Brendan: "So you should give me your number."

Me: (more nervous laughter, followed by me programming my number into his phone)

In retrospect, I have no idea why that comment had worked on me, or why my near-psychotic mannerisms worked on him…but whatever, we were in business.

A few days into our first semester, I came down with a cold. Maggie had to deal with my dramatic declarations that I was "going to die," Jenny had to hear me coughing across the hallway, and Hannah had to wake me up for my 8:00 AM class. Apparently, I made everyone around me miserable. So miserable, in fact, that when Maggie's parents invited me to the auditorium's production one evening, I really had to say "no thank you." I could not bear the thought of burdening someone with my intense coughing and fountain of a nose. Besides, I was convinced that this was the evening I was going to die.

I am so rational.

I was going to spend the night alone, planning my funeral, until my phone vibrated and flashed Brendan's number, with a text saying, "Hey what are you up to tonight?" I told him that I had planned to die of my sinus infection, and that I'd like to do so in peace. He informed me he was coming over. "Um... didn't you read? I am sick. Probably contagious and most likely with the plague," I told him as gently as possible. His response? "I'm part Mexican. We don't get sick."

Sounded legitimate to me!

I rushed into the bathroom and washed the sweat and snot off my face that had accumulated over the past few days. I threw off my frumpy sweats and changed into cute IU shorts and a tee. I added mascara to my eyes, foundation to the bags accompanying my eyes, and sprayed a small cloud of body spray around myself and my room. Then, I anxiously waited for him to arrive.

It was so casual of me.

And he did arrive in all of his tall, toned, tanned glory and settled himself in my hot pink and bright green dorm room. I had never had a boy in my room before. Ever. In high school, my parents would never even let boys upstairs in my house where my room was located! What does one do with a boy in their room? Offer them a cold beverage? Give them a tour? I was clearly perplexed by this "creature" or so-called-boy. Luckily, Brendan was a man of the world. He had clearly done this before – which, looking back, should not have been so comforting. "Why don't we put in a movie?" Brendan suggested. "Then you can come cuddle with me." Panic struck me to my conservative Catholic core. Now, not only was there a boy in my room, but he was interested in cuddling with me. Catholic school did not prepare me for this. So we popped in a movie, and I sat as far away from him as humanly possible in the

9-by-14 room that was predominately beds and clothes. "Is that your idea of cuddling?" he asked me.

Damn, he had figured me out.

It wasn't that I didn't want to cuddle with him. He was cute and really nice. It was my inner monologue that kept me from going over to him. "What if I don't know what to do? What if he is just kidding? What if he wants to kiss? When was the last time I kissed someone? What is he thinking? WHAT AM I THINKING?!" My brain was noisy with negative thoughts. Eventually, I inched forward to sit on the floor with him, and eventually he tried kissing me, and eventually I let him. It felt weird kissing in my over-lit, over-decorated, 9-by-14 dorm room. But this was college. So, I decided (as he was leaving) that I liked him and wanted to pursue a relationship with him. It really seemed like more of a logical step than a desire to be with him. When I explained to him that I had enjoyed myself and liked hanging out with him, he told me that he was having fun too and that he'd like to hang out again, but we should "…keep our friendship private…there is no need to post it all over Facebook."

Poor, naïve freshman Brittney.

Lesson Number Two Revisited: Stop having expectations, you

moron.

So I believed there would be a relationship, or at least a friendship. I kept calling and texting him, but it wasn't really going anywhere and I didn't understand why. He had said he had a good time, didn't he? And I had a good time too. So what was the problem?

It all came out when I asked Jenny about it.

I was sitting in her room, watching her get ready to cheer a basketball game one day when I finally approached her about Brendan.

"So…I really have a crush on Brendan…" I began, as I looked at her in the mirror, where she was applying her lipstick. The second I spoke, a look of panic hit her face.

"Oh…" Jenny's perfectly lined lips scrunched into a look of concern as I talked.

"Something you'd like to tell me..?" I noticed her giant baby blue eyes dart back and forth, trying to avoid my gaze in the mirror in front of us.

"Well…." Jenny began.

And that's when I began to see the fairy tale of my first college romance go up in flames.

"You know…he kinda…well they're not exactly…but it's kind of long-term…you know he has a girlfriend right?" she stammered, still avoiding my eyes in the mirror in front of us.

A girlfriend. The bastard had a girlfriend. He had certainly never mentioned THAT.

Well, there goes that so-called relationship – and along with it, my motivation to go to class.

Lesson Number 6: How to (almost) fail out of college (with a Bonus Lesson in pissing off your parents).

You see, I have the tendency to believe that I "deserve" time off. When I have had emotional distress, I believe I deserve a break. When things are tough, I feel that I should be allowed to relax without the interruption of school. The time that I took off after "The Brendan Issue" was pretty much the rest of the semester. I came home to Chicago in mid-December to find that my GPA for my first semester was a 1.49 and that I would be on academic probation in the spring.

Shit.

I spent the majority of my winter break begging my parents for forgiveness and for the opportunity to go back to school and prove that I could succeed. I had a complete attitude adjustment, signed up for better classes, and was ready to do the whole "college" thing again.

"You have no idea what we have sacrificed," my mom began, "for your education. Your father works hard to pay your tuition, we gave you everything you needed to succeed, and yet you were so disrespectful to not even try and give college a chance."

Damn she is good.

So, with a heavy heart and a ready mind, I headed back down to Bloomington.

Round Two. Ding ding ding! I was like a boxer heading back into the ring, armed with a pack of highlighters, a case of highly caffeinated Mountain Dew Code Red, and a new day planner.

Hell Yeah.

Lesson Number 7: How to Meet Cute Guys (with added degrees of difficulty)

I-65 is generally the road I take to the lovely B-Town. However, there was a severe snowstorm that day I drove back in 2009, and I-65 is not known for its excellent plowing during the winter. As a desperate last-minute move, my dad directed me down Illinois and over to Indiana, as opposed to across Indiana on I-65. My new route was going to take about an hour longer, but it was going to be safer. So I embarked on the journey with my iPod docked and ready to go, with groceries and fresh laundry in the back, and with a clear and refocused mind.

It took extra patience to drive that day, which gave me plenty of time to contemplate my wrongdoings of the past semester. I had a broken record of "things to do" this coming year in my head: more studying, more library time, no more oversleeping, no more going out, no more extracurriculars, and finally, NO MORE BOYS.

How optimistic of me...

I am always in my element when driving. There is something about the open road, me alone in the car, and my awesome selection of tunes that really relaxes me. Drives make me happy, they make me smile, and they give me the best feeling in the world. Drives give me drive.

Until, inevitably, I was stuck behind a semi-truck. Who really likes being stuck behind those? They go like 55 miles per hour and they always seem to pop up at the worst time. Then, I was stuck behind two semi-trucks with no way to get around them.

Then I was stuck behind those two semis, which were both stuck behind plow trucks. Crap, crap, crap.

Finally, I saw it – my opportunity to pass. The trucks cleared a path for me and I was ready to go. I sped up, I put my turn signal on, I changed lanes, and then…I was spinning.

The second I hit the ice, I knew I was not going to make it to the party I had planned on going to that night. The second I hit the pole that smashed in the side of my car, I heard my dad calling my cell phone wondering where I was at. The second I went into the ditch and into the fence, I knew I was in trouble.

I watched it all unfold before my eyes. I tried to change the course of the car, I swerved and spun, I prevented myself from hitting the pole head. I watched as cars stopped around me, as the glass of my windows shattered, and after that my eyes shut tight. I couldn't do it anymore. The sounds were enough for me. The wind rushing in the car, the screeching of the tires, and the splash as I hit the wet mud of the field below the highway told me that this was bad.

When the car came rolling to a stop, I finally took my hands off the wheel and opened my eyes. There was glass everywhere; the windows on the passenger side were completely busted. As cool air rushed into my car, my phone was still ringing.

"Daddy? Dad? Help! Oh god I am so sorry Daddy I crashed the car! Dad I am so sorry…" I screamed into the phone once I found it.

"Brittney, are you okay?"

"Yeah Dad but the car…oh God the CAR! Dad I'm in a ditch and…"

"But you are okay? You're not hurt?"

"I don't think so but...oh God somebody just got out of their car and told me they would call 9-1-1! Dad I can't get the keys out and the car is so cold and I don't know what is going to happen. Am I going to get a ticket? Am I going to jail? Daddy, help!"

"Hang on, okay? We're coming. Just hold on."

So I did. I found my coat and I walked around a little trying to calm down. I even hung out with the plow-truck guys until the ambulance loaded me up.

"What's your name, sweetheart?" the nice EMT asked.

"Brittney Little. Or Brittney Ann Little. I don't remember what my license says. My mom likes to use my middle name a lot...and I don't know why I am telling you all of this," I rambled on, clearly an idiot. I wondered if he thought I was in shock. Or maybe he would put me in a mental hospital. I seriously needed to stop rambling.

"And what's your phone number?"

"Cell or home?"

"Cell."

So I give it to him; without a rant or an over-explanation. Good self-control there, Bee.

"Great," the EMT said while laughing, "Now I have your number so I can call you."

Well, this just got a little more interesting.

I ended up in the hospital next to a family who was contemplating the legal issues of their loved one in the ER. On the other side of me was a man handcuffed to his chair. Awesome. The nice EMT walked over and handed me a sheet of paper, "This is my number and my name is Robbie. I think you're really cute and if you need anything, shoot me a text or give me a call."

The woman next to me looked at her daughter and said, "I guess chivalry and true romance still do exist."

All in all, my day was not so bad.

My parents ended up coming to get me, traveling back home, and then back to the lovely city of Danville to get my car in the morning. All the while, I got to text my new friend Robbie. When I told the story to my roommate and floor-mates, all was not lost. Because in the end, I had made a cute new friend! Sure, I had around $5,000 in damages to the car, but I had a cute new friend! I sure wish my parents had felt that way...

So the new semester began with a bang, literally.

Lesson Number 8: The ability of college to completely shoot down your dreams.

I was enrolled in a class to help with my "study skills" due to my less-than-stellar academic performance. The first class was a lecture about how arrest or court dates were the only excused absences. Wow –these were not my people. But the class ended up actually being helpful. The biggest focus of the course was goals and career ideas. My career idea: country music superstar. My course instructor's thoughts on that idea: "Ha ha ha."

Bummer.

I had dreamt of going to Nashville and becoming a country superstar since I was 6 years old, belting out "One Way Ticket" by LeAnn Rimes in my bedroom. Over the years the song has changed, but the dream has not. I guess this childhood dream was what held me back in college. I had always thought that I wouldn't need school, and I would just need to learn to write and play guitar. By the end of freshman year, however, I was realizing how unlikely that was going to be, and I needed to find something else to do.

List of Things I'd Like To Do Because Being a Country Music Superstar Is Seemingly Unattainable and I Need to Appease This Teacher So I Can Stop Being on Academic Probation

1) Write for Seventeen Magazine
2) Write for Cosmopolitan
3) Write a book
4) Write songs

Luckily, these all had a common theme: I would need practice writing.

So, my life was back on track. I was going to classes, I was hanging with friends, and I dared to say I was going to succeed that semester.

Until I saw him walking down the hallway.

Crap. Another boy.

He was tall, really skinny, not really my type, but he definitely had a nice smile. He was new on the floor and I had yet to meet him.

"Who is that guy going into our RA's room?" I tentatively asked Maggie one January afternoon.

"Um…that would be our new RA."

When you ask a stupid question…

After a few days on the dorm floor, we got to meet our new RA David, and were even invited to a party at his off-campus fraternity. Finally, yes FINALLY, the girls and I had somewhere to go out.

The whole floor was buzzing about the party. The girls were creating a new hole in the O-Zone layer with all the hairspray that was being sprayed as the boys were…well, whatever boys do when they get ready to go out. I had yet to REALLY go out in college. We had gone to events at the auditorium and the free movies at the student union, but not yet to an actual fraternity party.

I was such a lame freshman that first semester.

We did not go with the intention of drinking. We hadn't even planned on staying long. But the bartender of the fraternity was mixing up Long Island Iced Teas and it was love at first taste. Suddenly, all the girls from the floor had loosened up and were partying down! We all danced around; drawing the attention of the boys…we could not stop ourselves if we tried!

Lesson Number 9: How to meet guys (The Liquor Way)

At the end of the party, we crammed into the fraternity's driver's car, drunk, tired, and each of us complaining of aching feet. I had never experienced a fraternity's driving system and was convinced that the boy was doing it out of the kindness of his heart and not out of responsibility to the fraternity. Apparently, I was so convinced that he was doing us a favor that I gave him my number as a prize.

Awesome work, Drunk Bee.

It wasn't until I survived both Jenny and Maggie puking that night, and the hangover day that followed, that I got a text message from a number I did not know.

"Hey" it said.

I hate when I get texts that say "Hey." What the hell do you want? "Hey" is such a waste of a text. Send me more than three letters. Give me some sort of clue as to who I am talking to and why we are about to begin a conversation.

Either I really felt that way, or I was just really hungover. It was definitely one of the two.

So I replied, "Hey…um…who is this?"

"It's Jacob."

Well, that's freaking helpful. I had seriously drunk way too much the night before.

"I'm gonna need more help than that buddy…"

It turns out he was the nice fraternity driver that gave me a ride home the night before. He also explained to me that he was on a fraternity retreat and would much rather be texting a beautiful girl than paying attention to what he was supposed to be doing.

Jacob was a smooth talker.

Had I still had my long, fairy tale hair, I would have flung it around in a flirty manner and batted my eyes at Jacob when I saw him again. But now that my hair was gone, flirting was more difficult. Yet I was still successful (or the large amount of liquor I drank was successful), because at the next fraternity party he invited me to, I finally got to re-meet him and, eventually, kiss him.

And damn, was Jacob a good kisser.

We later found out we were in the same Math class and began to study for exams together. I later ended up getting a D in Math.

You can't win them all I guess.

Jacob was really everything I was not. He was a bit dangerous, a bit wild, and definitely more experienced in the ways of the world. How do these kinds of guys keep finding me? I had every intention of pursuing a relationship with him. But when do things go as I intend them to?

Friends from high school coming to visit IU's campus and see both Maggie and me. They, of course, were interested in partying and I, of course, had only one place to party. So it was back to David's off-campus fraternity. However, my lack of sleep, my lack of food that day, and the large amount of liquor I drank at the party, brought me to instant sickness. David offered to take me home. Then he offered to let me hang out in his room until my guests came back with my room key. Then he shoved his tongue down my throat. I was not exactly enjoying myself. But I was not exactly pushing him off.

Rough life.

I should have realized it then, with my eyes opened, staring at the dirty dorm room that I was in. that I really was not that interested. I'll blame it on my freshman naivety.

Later the next day, David asked me out on a date, and I said I would think about it. Things with Jacob were coming to an end, and I was really enjoying the newfound boy attention I was receiving from David. I had entered "The David Era."

It was a dark time, accompanied by another short haircut and several nights spent trying to figure out what he wanted out of me. We became pretty close, talking about everything, spending meals together, and suddenly I didn't find him so scary anymore. We could be friendly...or even more if we wanted to.

Lesson Number 10: How to ruin your freshman year in one simple party (with a bonus lesson: a how-to guide to moronic nicknames).

A few weeks after my friendship with David began, his fraternity held an "A-B-C Party" or an "Anything But Clothes" party. The directions are simple: cover yourself in anything but conventional clothes. I chose a bikini top with pink and orange stripes and borrowed tuxedo designed boxer shorts and headed out on the town with David and Hannah. The night was going to be another classic college night full of booze, boys, and good friends.

The bass was thumping, the boys and girls were dancing and the keg was tapped when we arrived. Oh yes, it was going to be a good night indeed. I danced with Hannah, I danced with David, and I even spent some time chatting with Jacob. Life was good, until Detroit walked in.

Detroit, of course, was not his real name. But apparently, since he was from Detroit, everyone felt the need to call him that. Anyway, he was friends with a few people on our floor, and I had met him a few times in my travels down the boys' hallway on my way to the laundry room. He came over to chat with me for a little bit and I just had a weird vibe about it...I mean I was there with David, I was talking to Jacob on the couch, and this guy came over to tell me that I "looked pretty damn good." It seemed a little strange to me, but I let it go.

Later in the night however, liquid courage hit him more. He was fingering my bikini top as he talked to me, rubbing his hands down my torso, and touching my face as he spoke. I politely asked him to stop and walked away. I tried to tell David and then I tried to tell Jacob, but I stopped myself. "You are an adult now," I told myself, "stop overreacting and just remove yourself from the situation."

In our third encounter, Mr. Detroit and I were destined to have a conflict. He and I were both drunk and while he had become more "handsy" with his liquor, I had become increasingly pissed off by his presence. He continued to rub his hands up and down my torso, touching my bikini top (and really anything he could get his hands on), until I told him to stop.

"Or what?" he questioned me.

"I'll give you three seconds to get your hands off me or I swear to God..." I began (slurring only slightly).

And before I knew it, I had hit him clear across the face.

I will never forget the look on his face after I hit him, just pure shock. His dirty lips rounded to a perfect "O" as he spat out "Oh my God." I don't think anyone saw that coming. I was just as surprised at myself as the people around me were. I caught a glimpse of the fraternity's bouncer's face, a slight smile before he 'bounced' into action. Detroit was thrown out of the party, and I was sent home to continue freaking out, being drunk, and crying in my own room.

However, the night was not over.

It could have ended at the fraternity. I could have let it go and not bothered Detroit ever again. I understood that people made mistakes or do did things without thinking much, especially when they were drunk. Sure, I could have left this incident in the past and moved on. But he was there when I got back to the dorm, and he could not contain his anger when he saw me. Hannah ushered me through his yelling, and I dashed straight past Maggie and Jenny into my own room to cry. Immediately, Maggie burst into our room after me.

"Brittney what happened? Are you okay?"

"I...I...I have to pee," I replied.

Smooth, right? I do well under duress.

So I dash down to the bathroom, now clad in a sports bra and shorts, and continue to cry in the stall. I barely realized that Maggie had brought me a tee-shirt to put on. I barely noticed that she and Hannah had followed me to see if I was okay. Or maybe just to be my bodyguards. Whichever.

Have I mentioned how awesome these girls are?

Back at our end of the hall (and finally out of the bathroom), I explained to Maggie and Jenny what had happened, with a few details added by Hannah and David. It felt good and safe to be out in the hallway with all of them, just relaxing. Maggie brought me a juice box from our fridge and teddy bears from our beds, and I began to calm down.

Until our friend Detroit returned to the floor.

He was short, he had a crew cut, and he was definitely a cliché. He wore a flat-billed baseball hat most of the time, baggy "Detroit" jerseys, and huge pants. In retrospect, he was nothing to be afraid of, but in that moment my freshman year, upon seeing him fear hit me before rationality did.

I raced into my dorm room and locked the door. Maggie blocked the hallway with her arms and words were exchanged between the two parties. All I did was cry.

I was such a wimp.

In the end of the night, I was calmed down and sent to bed. I thought it would be over. I thought everything was going to be okay after that.

When am I ever right?

A few days later Detroit stopped Jenny and I on our way to Tae Kwon Do class. He demanded to know why I had gotten him in trouble at the fraternity, yelled at me about the fact that I had gotten the RAs of our building involved, and told me, "I have seen girls like you. I would not touch a girl like you. Why would you tell people that?"

College was turning out to be so much fun.

So the "Powers that Be" (also known as my parents) gave me a few options.

I could come home. Ain't no shame in giving up after a semester like this.

I could switch dorms...we could figure something out.

I could call the police.

The first two options seemed like a lot of effort...so I picked "calling the police."

No, really, college was exactly what I had wanted it to be.

Detroit was eventually forbidden from coming to our floor and from trying to discuss things with me.

It was at this moment in my freshman year when I took a good look at my life. Maggie was being so nice, and even wrote me a letter telling me how strong I was and how I could totally get through this. Hannah took me off campus with her whenever she could, and Jenny was a great listener, even when I was rambling about the same things over and over again. It gave me strength, even when I thought I couldn't do it. I spent many nights afraid of the dorms and scared Detroit would return. I spent many mornings oversleeping, having meetings with the dorm's directors, and explaining my situation to my professors and lecturers. But my IU family became a group of people that I could depend on, and I hoped they could depend on me. We were a family, despite our terrible situations.

Freshman year was not even exceeding my ridiculously low expectations. How is that possible?

Lesson Number 11: How to make things seem more dramatic (or, a lesson in capitalization)

Eventually, things leveled out and life was okay again. I was still with David, although things were completely different after "The Detroit Incident."

That is what I refer to it as, all capitalized and everything. It was traumatizing, so it gets to be a proper noun.

Anyway, David became distant and demeaning and yet, he still wanted to spend time with me. And here comes the climax of "The David Era."

I Swear, Freshman Year Was Nothing But Capitalization.

It started small. A little comment here and there from him. For example, "I don't think anyone is going to be able to handle you. After the whole Detroit thing, you are way too emotionally damaged to even talk to."

David was precious.

Slowly though, he built up his confidence, as mine slowly diminished. I truly believed that he was the only person who could understand me and the only person who liked me. Gee, I wonder why.

"No guy would be as patient as me to deal with this shit," he mused one night as we were watching TV, "No seriously...you're a mess and you really aren't doing much with your life. How is the academic probation thing going for you?"

Where do I find these people?

He kept poking at my self-esteem, in addition to poking at my stomach and legs, criticizing my appearance along with my intelligence and dependence upon my friends and family. The worst part about it was that I thought it was normal. But after a few months of that, I realized I could be friends with him and nothing more. My mind was made up. And thus, I was single heading into Indiana University's "Little 500 Week."

Lesson Number 12: Party weeks require training (ladies and gentlemen, start your livers!)

IU's Little 500 Week is a magical (thought to be fictional) five (or more) days of pure partying. Classes get shortened or canceled, and those that aren't are a mess of absences and drunks. Students day drink, lay out and tan outside their dorms and apartments, and costumes are a must. Costumes? Yes, costumes. Little 500 is full of themed parties. Fraternities, apartment complexes, and individual houses all band together to intensely "live up" one of the final weeks of school.

Why all the partying? The week culminates in three races: Little

50 (a fifty lap running relay), Little 500 Women's Race (a bike race), and Little 500 Men's Race (also a bike race). It is the largest intramural competition in the nation. Guests like Barack Obama, Lance Armstrong, and Michael Phelps have attended this race. Little 500 Week/Weekend has been called "The World's Greatest College Weekend" (Seriously, I am not biased. Google that. Now.).

Each university has its claim to fame – "Unofficials," "St. Practice Day, "Grand Prix" – but nothing is as extraordinary as an entire WEEK of partying and school pride. Nothing is as unique as students training all year for this intramural race. There is nothing in this world as extraordinary as living through "The World's Greatest College Weekend." Nothing is quite as big, as important, as prestigious, as Indiana University's Little 500 Week. All of this magic hit me in the spring of 2009, when I was seriously single and seriously ready…bring on the booze.

Day One: I stayed up all night studying. FAIL. I needed to make up for lost time in the remaining days.

Day Two: I headed to David's fraternity's charity event for the evening to visit with my old friends. David had been there for a bit, but had to leave due to his RA responsibilities, so it was left to me and Hannah to entertain the boys.

Now we're talking.

Hannah was the "sober driver" that evening, so I was going wild. The "charity event" had long ended and the liquor had come out. As I grabbed a drink and chatted with a friend, a bald guy with a goatee walked on over.

"Brittney, do you know Michael?" my friend inquired.

No, I did not.

Lesson Number 9 Revisited: Meeting Guys The Liquor Way – a flawless approach

Michael and I got to talking, and flirting a little, and drinking a little more. A few whiskey sours later, my head was spinning and I needed to find Hannah.

"It was really nice to meet you," Michael said as he led me to the stairs.

"Yeah...I..." I began, and then he kissed me.

It was nice – it was unexpected, but it was nice – until Hannah appeared at the bottom of the stairs, summoning my drunken ass out the door and into her car.

Classy.

I woke up the next morning to a text from my new friend Michael, asking me to come over and visit him before he left. Michael was from Indianapolis, and only visiting Bloomington for Little 500 Week. He was built like a football player, with the darkest and most gentle brown eyes I had ever seen. He had giant arms to go with his giant smile and I figured I could learn to live with the goatee. Luckily, I would not have to.

"Well, I am heading to my recruiter to get my boot camp dates today," he said as we sat and talked.

Recruiter? Boot camp? He was in the military? Goodbye goatee, and hello even bigger muscles! Oh Lord, was I in trouble with this boy.

After spending the evening with Michael, and the morning with Michael, I had completely forgotten about David – until he was knocking at my door.

"I heard you had sex with my friend Michael," David spat at me.

"Well, hello to you too," I said, "Please, come in…" I managed to stammer, as he pushed past me into my dorm room.

"I just cannot believe that you would have sex with him after you just met him…you are such a slut!"

"Um. Excuse me? When did I sleep with him?"

Apparently, one of David's brilliant fraternity brothers saw me kiss Michael the previous evening, and then saw me leaving from my visit with Michael that next morning. This fraternity brother, however, did not stop to get more information.

I swear, sometimes boys can be so dense.

"No, you've got it all wrong," I had started to explain, when Hannah came in.

"I don't know where you got your information, or who you think you are talking to her like that," Hannah began in her usual spitfire fashion, "But last I checked I drove her ass home and took the bus with her to class early this morning. You might want to check your fucking facts the next time you come in here and accuse my friend of being a slut."

Did I mention that she rocks?

I saw Michael only one more time that semester, and then it was just a friendship of texting and mutual admiration. He was sweet, but he was leaving for boot camp in a few weeks and nothing was going to come of that relationship. But he was a nice guy, and he became my strength to get away from David for good and move on with my life. It was great to have someone understand, and even better to have someone that was available to talk to at any given moment. Who knew that one drunken night at a frat house I'd find one of my best friends?

A few rough weeks after Little 500, I was done with freshman year…no. That is not the best way to describe it. I had SURVIVED freshman year. I had endured drunken boys, police action, dumb boys, and all while sharing a tiny dorm with an equally confused college freshman. I began looking at my college experience and realized I had become a cautionary tale. Brittney Little, showing people what NOT to do in their first year of school. Yes, that was me at the end of my freshman year, but I was ready for change.

Lesson Number 13: Idle hands are the devil's playthings

Summer was really uneventful. For starters, I had one part-time job at a dance apparel boutique. I basically spent my days ringing up leotards, tights, and ballet shoes and fitting picky girls for new apparel, while also dealing with their stage mothers. I was paid eight dollars an hour to be the only person in the hot and sticky store, and I spent 80 percent of the time reading and daydreaming about my sophomore year.

It was during one of those blazing summer days at the dance store that a dream of mine began to unfold. I had not danced in quite some time, having taken a break from it in high school, and I longed for another opportunity to perform. Indiana University had *some* options for performers:

Redsteppers: a "precise" kick team that dances during football season alone. The Redsteppers wore red dresses, white gloves, and cowboy boots. Maggie became a Redstepper and really enjoyed it. While the Redsteppers enjoyed high visibility at football games and were given prime performances, the team's choreography and fashions were not really for me.

Cheerleading: Jenny was an IU cheerleader. Everything about the team was amazing. The girls could perform intense stunts and tumbling maneuvers all while wearing beautifully crafted cheer uniforms, but they were not dancers, which was something I craved to be again.

Hoosier Dance Team: A club dance team on campus that aimed to compete, and not much more. The girls were technically perfect; however, the commitment was huge. Not only did practices and performances consume their lives, there was a high financial responsibility attached to joining the team.

In order to perform in the uniforms, with the choreography, and at the commitment level I wanted, I would have to make it happen myself.

Why is everything always up to me?

With all of my spare time to plan and scheme, the Indiana Hoosierettes Pom and Dance Team was born.

It was also at that point that someone should have had me committed. Clearly, in taking on a student organization, I was nuts.

I spent hours planning out cheap uniforms and figuring out how to become a legitimate team on campus. All of this was happening in the summer before my sophomore year, and all while I was trying to balance my daydreams of a better year of college and becoming a "new person."

It was worth a shot.

Fool Me Twice: Sophomore Year

I'll admit that freshman year was not me in the best light at all. Then again...all of college probably wasn't. You would think I had learned my lesson...but I went out and got another short haircut before I headed back to school for my sophomore year.

The good news for sophomore year was that I was no longer in that hellhole of a dorm. I had moved on and moved in to a brand new townhouse with Jenny and two of her cheerleading friends. The townhouse was magical. It was sleek and modern, with a giant living room complete with faux leather couches and armchairs, a coffee table, and a flat screen television. The kitchen had granite countertops, a beautiful bar, and faux (but still classy) hard wood floors. We were in the most luxurious accommodations that Bloomington had to offer. From the day I moved in, sophomore year was going to be fabulous.

I really needed to stop having any kind of expectations where college was concerned.

Lesson Number 14: Don't hang on to the fraternity boys

Before I could leave for Middletown to pick up Hannah and help her move her things, I was summoned to see the fraternity's new house. As I pulled in the driveway in my denim sundress and gold sandals, I had a rush of nostalgia for the boys I had come to know so well over the past year. I had missed them in the past months, and could not wait to see them. I adjusted my gold pendant around my neck, grabbed my wallet, and stepped out onto the hot pavement, and straight into the arms of Jacob.

Oh yeah. I was about to get myself in all kinds of trouble in my sophomore year.

I tentatively made my way through the house, dodging boxes, furniture, and fraternity brothers. I found my way through and up to Jacob's room, where a few of the brothers waited to start their "roommate meeting." It is such a boy thing to ask a girl to help them write out their chore charts and their house rules, but I was not put out by the request. My roommates and I did not have a similar set of rules and I wondered if the boys had the right idea. Should the cheerleaders and I set out some rules? Nah.

Oh, when will I learn?

Lesson Number 15: How to get off to a rough start with the new roommates.

After moving Hannah in to her new townhouse, we decided to invite Jacob and some of the brothers over to my new place to play some drinking games. When I texted Jenny to tell her my plans to have people over, she replied that she and Hayley, our other roommate, had already planned to have people over.

I am the first person to admit that text messaging is difficult to decipher. Meanings can be skewed without a tone. On one hand, Jenny could have meant that we were going to have a big and fun party…but what it sounded like to me was that their friends were coming over. so mine couldn't. When I texted Jacob to un-invite him and the boys and told him the reason why, he replied, "Oh no. This is not going to be like this all year for you. We'll show them. See you in a bit."

I had no idea what that meant.

So Hannah and I traveled back to my townhouse to wait. We began drinking, we began loosening up, and Hannah's friends began to show. It wasn't terrible, but it was not comfortable. Hannah and I began taking shots of Skyy vodka, mixing up drinks, and staring awkwardly at Hayley's friends. to whom we were not introduced at all. We were the "awkward guests" (even though it was my house too), but we were slowly getting buzzed, so it really did not matter. A few shots in, my cell buzzed on the now sticky countertop.

"Hello?"

"Hey…we're here," Jacob said before hanging up.

As I peered out the front door, I had realized what Jacob had meant. He had rallied up several of his fraternity brothers and the troops were heading up my front steps to take over the party.

Oh my goodness.

After several uncomfortable stares from Hayley and Jenny's crew, Jacob and the boys packed their booze, our booze, and Hannah and I into their SUV.

"Where are we going?" I managed to slur from the back of the car.

"To get our own party started," Jacob replied.

Being stolen from your own apartment and taken across town should be scary, but, apparently, I was having the time of my life. We drank more, laughed more, and eventually, I was sent to bed in someone else's house.

"wher d you goe?" I managed to drunk-text Hannah.

"Sweetie, YOU went to BED," was her response.

"But I haftda peee," I responded, apparently incredulous that I was secluded in some room far away.

I am such a classy drunk.

The next morning, I could not find Hannah to save my life. I knocked on the doors of many rooms in the house, asked around, and was eventually sent home with one of the fraternity brothers.

"Oh. Hey." Hannah texted me back after I called her 4 or 5 times.

Sweet timing, Hannah.

So I drove back across town to get her from the boys' house and, in such a timely manner, Kenny Chesney's "We Went Out Last Night" was playing as she walked out the door.

"We went out last night," Kenny crooned, "like we swore we wouldn't do. Drank too much beer last night…a lot more than we wanted to…"

And even from ten feet away at the front door, I saw that Hannah and I had burst into giggles at the song at the exact same time.

Oh yes, sophomore year had officially begun.

The Sunday night before the first day of school I am always a wreck. I panic about ordering books, I freak out about new teachers and classrooms, and I simply cannot sleep. The Sunday night before my sophomore year, I had similar worries until I received a phone call.

"Hello?" I asked tentatively to the unlisted phone number.

"Brittney?" a deep male voice answered.

"Yeah…"

"It's Michael!" he replied.

I had gotten a phone call from Michael at his Army training camp.

Well, that put me in a good mood!

After a phone call that ended too quickly for my taste, I was soothed to bed to dream of cute boys in Army uniforms.

And man, did I have some sweet dreams that night.

Lesson Number 16: How to make a good impression (The Liquor Way)

The next morning, I woke up to find that my grape juice was gone, meaning that I had no drinks of my own to have with breakfast. Damn! *But what is this?* I thought to myself. *Hannah left a red Powerade in the refrigerator from our party a few days ago!* Now, I had never been a Powerade kind of gal, but I was desperate for something to drink with breakfast and figured Hannah would not mind if I polished off the beverage. So I poured myself a glass, and it was surprisingly tasty. It almost felt warm going down, which I thought was strange, but I ignored the thought and poured the rest of the drink into my coffee thermos and headed off to class.

While sipping on the drink all day, I found myself incredibly bubbly. I was talking to everyone, and making friends with all of my new classmates. In my second class, I found out that my good friend TJ was enrolled in the class as well.

"Hey!" I said brushing his arm as I spoke, "How are you? We are in the same class! How cool!"

"Hey," he growled back in his signature deep voice.

We continued to chat, and I continued to feel the need to touch his arm unnecessarily until he asked,

"Are you drunk?"

Drunk. It finally clicked. I hadn't been drinking pure Powerade all day; I had been drinking the Powerade that we had mixed the leftover vodka with.

Oops.

Well, that certainly explained my cheeriness, friendly nature, and my inability to walk in a straight line.

Yes, indeed, sophomore year had begun.

In the next few weeks, I continued to get phone calls from Michael every Sunday, continued to stay away from Powerade, and begin to fall into the rhythm of college. Finally, my life was normal.

For about three weeks or so, anyways.

It was about to happen. I knew it was a big deal because my apartment was clean, my sheets were fresh, I was showered, shaved, and anxiously awaiting the arrival of someone very special.

That's right. Lizzie was finally come visit Bloomington!

My best friend in the whole wide world had yet to meet all of my B-town friends, had yet to see the fraternity house, and had yet to get falling-over-drunk with me.

After some directional difficulty (that's my fancy way of saying she got her ass lost in Indianapolis), Lizzie arrived in all of her strawberry blond, perfectly made-up, and excellently dressed glory. The screams and squeals of delight as we were finally reunited could probably be heard throughout the entire city of Bloomington and its surrounding counties. We giggled, chatted, drank, and, of course, spent time at the fraternity house the first night. I wanted her to meet all of my new friends and she did. Lizzie is so easy to bring around...like I said, she could befriend anyone.

Lesson Number 17: How NOT to party right

The second night of her stay, Lizzie and I got all dressed up, picked up Hannah, and, as usual, headed to our off campus fraternity. Hannah and I were making the rounds saying "hello" and introducing Lizzie to anyone and everyone. We drank a little, danced a little, and before we knew it, the liquor had run out.

Party foul.

As resourceful people do, Hannah came up with a solution to the problem. She would walk back to her house, get a few beers and a bottle of vodka, and head back to the party with her cousin, Aiden, acting as her protection.

Lesson 17.1: Never retrieve your own stash of liquor after the party booze runs out.

I hadn't really realized how drunk Hannah actually was. I was too busy looking across the room at the cloud of darkness that had arrived. That's right – my old flame David was back, and he had brought his new girlfriend.

After my freshman year, I tried to remain friends with David. I asked him once how his summer was and the conversation ended with me in tears. I was convinced that I could fix our problems, and that he and I could become friends again.

I had conveniently forgotten that he was such an asshole.

So there he was, and there I was, at the same party. I'll admit I was a little buzzed, and still a little wrapped up in my crush on Jacob, but I was determined to befriend David. So I walked up to him and said "hello," asked how he was doing, and what was new.

He looked at me like I had five heads, said "Huh? I have no idea what you're talking about," and then walked away.

Can't say I didn't try.

I went back to Jacob's house across the lawn to grab my purse, adjust my makeup, and find someone to chat with. I had a few minutes to relax by talking to Jacob, when I realized I had completely ditched Hannah and Lizzie.

Oops.

By the time I headed back down to the "party house," all hell had broken loose. For starters, Hannah was the most drunk that I had ever seen anyone, ever. Her eyes were glassy and small, she could barely hold herself up, and she kept laughing. Not that she was laughing at anything in particular; she would just stare at you and laugh every few minutes. Poor Lizzie was busy downstairs caring for her, and brilliantly suggested that we should take Hannah home.

Seemed like a simple enough solution.

So I stomped over to the president of the fraternity, with Lizzie and Hannah in tow, to plead our case. Since Hannah was such a mess, he said he would help us find a ride, but they did not have an assigned sober driver for the evening. As I sent Lizzie and Hannah over near the driveway with Aiden aiding them, I watched Hannah walk into a tree and say,

"Ohmigosh I am so sorry."

It was truly going to be a challenge getting her home that evening.

When I turned back to the house to retrieve our stuff, David was standing there with his arms spread by the doorway, blocking the entrance to the house.

"Um…I have to get in there." I said.

"That's not a good idea," he replied, "You know why."

"Well...my purse is in there, Hannah's purse is in there, and I am not sure if you noticed but she is a hot mess. I am trying to get her home and I can't do that without her keys..." I began, while watching him shake his head.

But before he could protest more and before I could finish my rant, Lizzie swooped in, grabbed my arm, and pushed past David into the house.

I have the best friends ever.

As we got into the car with everyone's personal items and one hammered Hannah, I directed the driver to her house.

"She lives at 14th and Lincoln, and thank you," I said to the driver that evening.

Aiden, however, had a different suggestion.

"It's more like 14th and Dunn..." he began. An argument commenced. Finally, I looked over at Hannah.

"Hannah, honey," I began as sweetly as I could, as her glassy eyes struggled to focus on mine, "What street do you live on?"

"President," Drunk Hannah slurred in response.

There is no President Street in Bloomington, and everyone in the car was perplexed, until I said, "Which president sweetie?"

"Lincoln."

Bingo.

Lesson Number 18: Always pay attention when the sober driver is taking you home.

We got Hannah home, but we managed to miss both of our turns on the way back to my townhouse. I had bigger issues on my mind, as I was worried about the situation with David. Why had he been so rude? Why was I not allowed to enter the house? I had tried texting him, but I got no response. What was his problem? I needed to know what I did wrong and I needed to change it. I emailed him in the hope that things would get better, but they got so much worse. Again, David refused to take my version or my witnesses version of the story and keep his own, the facts be damned.

Apparently, according to him, I had "tried to fight his girlfriend" by throwing my shoulder into her and yelling obscenities at her. During the time I was allegedly fighting this girl, though, I was talking to Jacob upstairs and trying to find Hannah a ride home in real life. So either his story was wrong, or I had figured out how to be in two places at once – and while the latter option seems way more exciting, it was truly unlikely.

Something was wrong here.

I was told to stop drunk texting, I was told to stop talking, and I was told that I was horribly out of line. I was told that "if you're going to be my friend then you have to be held to a higher standard... meaning when you do things that are stupid, I don't want to be around you." And that it was his fraternity, not mine and it was pathetic that I was, "trying to hook up with them [his fraternity brothers] so that you can come by the house... that's my house. You wanna come, fine, I don't care, but do not make me or my friends uncomfortable because honestly you may not realize you're doing it but you are trying to go out of your way to make other people uncomfortable... back off and if you didn't know this you are trying to make other people uncomfortable at my house and it makes you a failure so stop fucking around!"

Gotta love that I could use direct quotes here.

Lesson Number 19: Keep the evidence.

And seriously, where do I find these people?

After begging, pleading, and even admitting to and apologizing for things that I didn't do, I stopped myself, took a step back, and realized: I'm too good for this.

I never consider myself conceited. I never, ever think of myself above anyone else. But in this situation, with this guy (who, by the way, was showing off his scrawny body on campus that semester in a "oh-so-classy" wife-beater and a trucker hat… how the hell had I ever found him attractive?), I had realized…he wasn't worth it.

It was a liberating feeling, finally being free from him. I was finally my own person. There I was, sitting in a dorm food court studying, and I realized that I didn't need to be anything for any guy. I just needed to be the best Brittney I could be. And that's when I came up with the mantra,

"I'm going to continue to be me with or without your approval. Why? Because being me is a pretty damn good thing."

Realization: complete. And it was finally strong enough to stick this time.

Being me truly WAS a good thing, and with my newfound confidence, I began to work on making my first college dream a realization: The Hoosierettes Dance Team.

Upon looking at the project, I knew it was going to be a lot of work. It was time to add on another mantra:

"One step at a time."

Step One: Meet with the Student Activities Office to become a legit team (so easy).

Step Two: Meet with the Athletic Department (not so easy).

I emailed every athletic director in IU athletics. I was really interested in getting this team started and seeing if we could perform at any IU athletic events. Without the promise of that, creating this team would be useless.

I met with Senior Athletic Director, who was interested in my idea of having more student involvement in athletics, and the meeting went great. He told me that in order to perform at athletic events, the dance team would have to become an IU athletic team, but my ideas brought the issue up in a positive light. I was told to begin the team and contact the Athletic Department the following fall.

Sweet deal.

It wasn't too long after my meeting with the Athletic Department that football season began. Football is seriously the best part about going to a Big 10 school. Although at the time Indiana's football team was not the greatest, our tailgating skills remained top notch.

I just remember sitting there, watching the Hoosiers play and thinking that this is what college was all about. I had my friends, I had my beers, and I had football. It was a classic college moment. Life at that point was going smoothly. Life was great.

But I should really learn that at these points, I should watch my back, because a few days later I woke up and something was wrong.

Very wrong indeed.

Lesson Number 20: Do you have medical insurance?

I suffered from stomachaches all summer and during the beginning of my sophomore year. I had tried everything: giving up lactose, giving up gluten, taking pills before I ate. Nothing seemed to help. But on this particular morning I was suffering from something totally different. It wasn't my stomach exactly, it was my side, and I was having issues keeping my composure or even thinking about going to class.

As every smart college student does in a crisis situation, I called my mommy.

We (more like she) decided that I should take some ibuprofen and head to my "History of Rock and Roll" class. I loved that class. It was located in a huge, well air conditioned auditorium where I sat in the front row and watched a really cool older guy rant with incredible passion about rock stars of the 1970's and 1980's. Twenty minutes into the class that day, however, the pain in my side began to hurt more and more. The room was suddenly too hot, the teacher could not go fast enough, and I was in a state of panic. I pulled out my phone and texted Jenny.

Twenty minutes later I was in Jenny's car on my way to Bloomington Community Hospital.

The place smelled sterile and the nurses looked busy and for a split second I thought about leaving until...oh yeah, I was in pain. So I signed in, sat myself down, and waited.

The waiting is always the worst part.

I was surprisingly calm for how unfamiliar I was with this degree of pain. They asked for some samples, poked around my sides and eventually told me I had kidney stones. Kidney stones. I was 19 and I had kidney stones.

What a life.

I'd eventually survive to pass my kidney stone, but it really made me wonder. Here I was, 19 and feeling like I was stuck in a 53 year old's body. What other health problems did I have that were going unnoticed?

I'm great at worrying too much.

But I continued to live my life by partying, going to class, and basically doing the whole "college" thing.

Lesson Number 21: Setting yourself up for failure (or, falling in love with fame)

In October, I had the amazing opportunity to perform a few of the songs I had written on the radio. My friend Brett worked for his college's radio station and had offered me an hour-long time slot. So, I headed to the studio with my guitar and my book of songs. I wore a flannel shirt, skinny jeans, cowboy boots, and glasses. Even though nobody but Brett would see me, I did my make-up nice and lightly glossed my lips. I was "performance ready." I sat in front of a legit radio microphone, with my "fans" (also known as Lizzie and my parents) visible through a window in the room behind us. Brett interviewed me in between my songs and played songs that had inspired my music career to give me a break from playing and singing.

This was my first taste of fame and I was ravenous for more. I loved performing, I loved being asked about my life and my music, and I loved everything about that day. I came out of that hour-long set so inspired and ready to do more. That day held everything that I had wanted to do for the rest of my life. All I needed was to perform. All I needed was my guitar and my lyrics.

It was one of my favorite things I experienced in college. I wanted more. Still want more. It was my first dose and I have remained hooked ever since.

Meanwhile, things with Jacob slowly ended (probably because he started dating someone else), but things with Michael started heating up. I was no longer getting only a phone call once a week. He had his cell back, he had his life back, and he was back in Indianapolis wanting to come and see me.

But suddenly, it was all a little too real.

Don't get me wrong, I loved talking to Michael. I had contemplated the situation I was in with him quite often. He was sweet, understanding, and oh yeah...cute. It was just that having him come an hour to see me was a lot. I didn't know what I wanted, I didn't know what he wanted, and the scariest thought of all was what if it all ended and I lost a good friend AND a guy I liked?

My brain just never quits.

Lesson Number 22: A Lesson in Math

Friendship + Love = Great

Friendship − Love and Relationship = No Friendship

But despite my worries, Michael did come to visit and I led him down the stairs at the townhouse into my bedroom. It was funny to see an Army guy sitting on my pink comforter under a wall full of ballet shoes and pictures of me and my high school friends. Surprisingly though, it wasn't awkward. This was the guy who wrote me letters telling me he missed me and all about boot camp. This was the guy who called every Sunday, even if it was just to listen to me complain about David or school. He had become my best friend and I hadn't even realized it.

Which of course, made the whole situation ten times scarier.

So I padded around him in my room in my slippers, nervous as hell, asking questions, chatting, offering him a soda from my mini fridge, until finally I made eye contact with him and he pulled me in tight for a kiss.

Oh. I had forgotten how nice that was.

And so, as I tend to do, I fell for him hard. He came to visit Bloomington a lot in those few weeks before finals and I started to feel like I was in a real relationship.

But I wasn't. And here's why:

I was way too clingy as a sophomore. I figured that out after David, and yet, with Michael, I could not stop myself.

We drank a lot together. I couldn't handle emotions and booze. I tended to say the dumbest things to him, with liquor to blame. Did I mean that I wanted to date him the night that we drank the whiskey? Probably. Did I mean to say it in that way and on that night? Probably not.

He didn't like me that much.

Okay so he did like me at one point. He liked me a lot, until he actually had me. Then it wasn't so much fun. One night we went to the movies and I had given him his Christmas present (Tim McGraw cologne and a fuzzy blanket). We were holding hands in his car when he kind of blurted it out.

He didn't think that we had any chemistry.

Of course, I was crushed. He promised that maybe things could change; that he wanted to love me and that I was really special to him. All I wanted was to go home and go to bed. I ran back into my apartment and collapsed onto the floor in a blurry mess of tears and smudged mascara.

The thing that sucks about mixing friendship with romance is that when the romance part tears you up, you want the friendship part to fix it. Both parts involve the same person so you love and hate him (or her) at the same time. And that was the situation I was stuck with. I wanted him to fix everything but I really hated him for hurting me too. He texted me and told me that he was sorry and that he still wanted to see me before I went home for break, so the next day I drove myself up to Indianapolis for a visit.

Looking back, I was desperate. My original instinct to stop trying and just be friends with Michael was right. But I was young, I guess, and upon visiting I still felt like nothing had changed, or maybe I had hoped nothing had. In that visit, I got to meet his family and see his home and it only convinced me more that we should be together.

How many times in my life will I say, "When will I learn?"

So we went along, pretending like nothing had changed (or maybe I was the only one that did), and I drove my car through Indianapolis and back to Chicago for Christmas break.

Christmas at home almost always feels magical. My mom is an expert decorator and our house has red and green nutcrackers, tiny lights, and garland everywhere. The tree in our living room looks like it came straight out of a Macy's store window, with all of the ornaments matching and ribbons everywhere. Back when my brother and I were little, our tree consisted of our homemade ornaments and little things from over the years. But by college, those had been long stored away in favor of the "classy" tree. However, during my sophomore year, my dad had taken out our old tree and decorated it with our old ornaments upstairs in our loft. The loft sits above the kitchen and is kind of our "upstairs basement." The loft housed our computer, pool table, barstools, and that Christmas, one of our trees. In addition to being an amazing decorator, my mom is a phenomenal cook. So, sitting in the loft with my special Christmas tree I could easily smell every cookie, every pie, every lasagna, and every ham that was cooked in preparation for Christmastime.

I was living the good life.

So I spent most of my break up in that loft, feeling the warm air rise, smelling whatever delicacy was in the oven, reading, and texting Michael. He was on his way to Florida with his family, so I was trying to play it cool, but I couldn't help but notice that he was acting kind of strange.

Lesson Number 23: How to get someone to dump you (The Annoying Way)

"How's it going hun?" I'd text.

"Fine," he would descriptively respond.

"Having fun yet?"

"Sure."

Ladies and Gentleman, I give you Michael, The Amazing Conversationalist.

Goodness.

I am ashamed to say, I began to bug him. I asked daily if everything was okay, then twice a day, then whenever he would text me. Then finally, at 3 A.M. on Christmas morning, I got my answer:

I don't like you, stop bothering me.

More or less, that was what he said. More or less, I began sobbing my eyes out.

I could see a little, at this point, why he was annoyed.

So after Christmas I did what every girl did when a boy broke her heart, I went and got a haircut. Selena Gomez (my new favorite Disney Channel celebrity) had gotten a chic bob haircut and I knew I had to have it. Forget that I had blond hair and not deep brown like Selena's, forget that my hair is probably the finest and thinnest hair on this planet, and forget that I did not really like my hair that short. I was going to do it.

I had yet to learn my lesson.

So I was going to start 2010 a brand new woman. I was seriously single and I had serious new hair. 2010 was going to be my year.

But first I had to survive New Year's Eve.

Lesson Number 24: How to get outrageously hungover

For Christmas that year I had gotten the "Magic Bullet" mini-blender and was going insane with the anticipation of trying it out. The manual had several recipes for smoothies, salsas, and a section titled "adult beverages."

Bring on the booze.

Hannah came all the way to Chicago to visit. We had a pretty boring night planned for New Year's Eve, since we were going to stay in all night. Mainly, we planned to use the "Magic Bullet" to make a drink called "Bullet to the Head" while watching television. We mixed vodka, gin, light tequila, and rum up with ice and cola in the blender and sucked a few "Bullets to the Head" down.

Ahhh.

When midnight came, we were barely aware and screaming in my living room. When my parents came home from a party around 2 A.M., we were so drunk we barely remember that. My mom gave us both brownies she had made for the party and sent us to bed...well, she sent me to bed. Hannah remained on the couch.

We spent our first day of 2010 outrageously hungover.

I should have known then that 2010 was not going to be my year either.

After our epic hangover (the hangover which will forever be referred to in hushed, reverent tones), Hannah and I both found ourselves back in Bloomington ready for the second semester of our sophomore year to begin. We each had a list of things we wanted to accomplish that semester, and number one on my list was the Hoosierettes Dance Team.

But first, I would fall back into the arms of Michael once more.

I really couldn't help myself. Well...maybe I could. But "will-power" is not my middle name. Again, he and I spent some time "fake dating." We visited one another, had dinners together, occasionally made out or watched television cuddling...I could learn to live like that. Right?

Wrong.

Lesson Number 25: How to get dumped (The Liquor Way)

One night, Michael came to Bloomington and we had plans to head to our old hang out, the fraternity house. There was going to be a big party there, and Hannah and I were itching to go, so I dragged Michael along. We got there and separated: Hannah and I went one way and Michael went the other. Before we knew it, Hannah and I were both wasted. One redhead, one blond, completely bombed.

That should have been our motto that year.

The bartender had cut me off after a while and I was on a rampage...how DARE he cut ME off? Did he know who I WAS?! And then I walked straight into Michael.

No literally, I almost did not see him and tripped and fell into him.

He was not nearly as drunk as I was, and the look of concern on his face told me I would not remember most of the night when I woke up. I was "drunk-girl stumbling" in my leather boots with chunky heels and I became more and more aware that I was going to humiliate myself in front of my dear friend Michael. Again.

Crap.

Some generous fraternity boy drove me to Hannah's where I panicked. I had lost Michael! I was texting him but due to the insane amounts of Everclear, rum, and beer I had had...he did not quite understand me. Eventually he paid the driver to come get me and bring us both home. He was being such a sweetheart.

I was not.

I did not remember a single thing from the time I got home, until I woke up at 6 A.M. vomiting everything up. Apparently, in that time I had taken a shower, made macaroni and cheese, and yelled at Michael for merely speaking to another girl. I later remembered him rubbing my back as I threw up, holding my hair back, and (even though he seemed annoyed at the situation) listening to me while I cried about it all. Other than that, the entire night was a complete blank, so I wondered why he was really mad at me the next morning. He didn't make eye contact with me after he woke up and didn't even want to hug me when he walked out the door.

I was in all kinds of trouble and I had no idea why.

He and I had signed up for a beer pong tournament the next weekend and I was still planning on him coming. I had spent the next few days worried he wouldn't come out of anger, but finally he texted saying he would be there, easing my fears. When the tournament came however, he never showed up. I went to the tournament and waited, eventually played with someone else, and left in tears.

It was really over.

I tried to talk to him a few times after that…but the conversations either ended with me in tears or with him ignoring me. After those days, things just kind of ended. I had no idea what I had done to receive that treatment and I had wished he would just talk to me.

Valentine's Day was coming up. I was heading out of town, and I was glad to bid Bloomington goodbye for a while. My parents had sprung for airplane tickets to fly me home for the weekend and avoid any weather issues while driving, and I soon found myself in the comfort of air travel.

And man, do I love to fly. I love wearing comfy-chic clothes and hanging out in the terminal. I love watching all kinds of people walk by. I love eating airport food, shopping in the little shops, and scoping out men in uniform. Yes, I am the kind of weirdo who lives for departure times, tidy flight attendants, and layovers.

I know. I am a freak.

After surviving the weekend at home, I was headed back to Bloomington. I relaxed in Midway Airport in Chicago wearing my Valentine's Day best: a pink thermal long sleeved tee, a denim mini, black knit tights, my Valentine's socks, and my hot pink UGG boots. I spent a little time during that day feeling sorry for myself that I had lost Michael, and generally sad that I was single. I began to feel even worse, until a cute guy sat down next to me on the plane.

Lesson Number 26: How to move on (The Cute Boy Way)

He was cute, but definitely older than I was, and he was heading to IU's law school where he attended. We had a great time talking and laughing on the plane. He was smart, he was worldly, and he was interesting. On paper he was perfect, but through all of that I knew he was not my type. We hung out on the bus to Bloomington and exchanged numbers, but nothing really came of it.

But I swear there is nothing like one boy to get over another boy.

Armed with my new confidence, I began working harder than ever on school and on Hoosierettes. I got a team of about six girls together, but it was too late in the year to really get things started. I would have to wait and work hard on it for the next year, and that was exactly what I did. I signed the group (meaning myself and my "team manager" Hannah) up for the school's annual "Student Involvement Fair" the following fall and made a Facebook page for the team. In no time, I had current and potential students interested in the group and I was very excited for the following year.

Before we all knew it, it was Little 500 Week again. It always seemed to sneak up on me.

Then, soon after Little 500, finals ensued and then summer began. I was broke and was in need of a job and with the economy in a state of "deflation," not a soul was hiring.

Lesson Number 27: How to use a job you hate, to get a job you love.

When I was sixteen, I had worked at a local golf course and had hated the job, but loved the money. So my mom convinced the owner to give me another shot, and I found myself up at 5:00 A.M. cleaning out golf carts for the second time in my life, and four years older this time.

What a lucky girl I was.

I had made the decision to be a better person that summer. I was going to have a positive attitude and be the best minimum wage worker they had. I distributed golf carts with a smile, prepared for golf outings with cheer, and even manned the grill stations with heart.

Customers were required to sign the golf carts out before riding them through the course. When one particular customer came up, I asked him to sign the sheet, please.

"I'll sign anything for you sweetheart," the guy joked.

"But will you sign my tuition checks? 'Cause if you'd do that, I probably wouldn't have to work here anymore," I joked as he drove the cart away.

When he came back, I asked (as I usually did) how the course was today and how he was doing.

"You know," he said to me, "You have a great personality."

"Thank you?" I said, unsure of the direction this conversation was heading.

"Are you looking for another job?" he asked.

Um. DUH. I am wearing a sky blue polo covered in stains of beer and cigar shavings, I spent my days sucking up to my fellow workers who were mainly under the age of 18, and if I wasn't quick enough for some of the old guys who golfed every evening they would run over my toes. Of COURSE I was looking for another job.

As it turns out, he was the owner of a very popular bar on the south side of Chicago. He was basically giving me a job based off of my personality alone.

How could I resist?

So, instead of spending the rest of my summer covered in stale beer that dripped from the golf carts and smelling of garbage juice, I was going to spend my summer working at a bar, making tips, and talking to customers.

Life was going to become so much better, I thought.

Why do I keep jinxing myself like that?

I was trained by four different waitresses, each with their own idea of what was important to learn and what was not necessary to remember. I made flashcards to learn the menu, I worked hard at understanding the different kinds of alcohol, and I even kept trying to befriend the other waitresses and waiters. I thought that this was the perfect job for me.

One of the managers loved me. He told me that I had such a great personality and that I was a ton of fun to have around. Who doesn't like someone who compliments you like that?

One of the managers thought I was "cute" and that I was a very hard worker. She praised me for staying late to learn closing procedures, helped me learn the computer system, and let me stay late to shadow other waiters and practice taking orders.

The top manager did not seem to like me very much. She said that I didn't "have it" to be a waitress and while she would always soften the blow with things like "you have a great personality though" or "keep trying," the words never sounded sincere. When most waitresses split up work like polishing silverware and cleaning things in the kitchen, this manager made me do them alone. I didn't take it personally and I tried not to dwell on it, but the staff I worked with noticed. I kept fielding questions about why this manager seemed to hate me and why, when this manager was working, was I expected to do certain things by myself.

I wanted to know too. But I kept my complaints to myself.

One night, I was permitted to do the "beer tubs." It was the best job ever. Being a "beer girl" is like opening a lemonade stand in the middle of a bar. Only, instead of lemonade, you're selling beer and offering a shorter wait than if you were to purchase the beer at the bar. There were a few bachelors' parties at the bar that night, and after clearing them out and making around $200 in tips I realized:

I would be a great bartender.

Unfortunately for me, that would be the last night that the managers gave me the beer cart. Suddenly, my hours were cut down more and more. When I asked the top manager why, she told me that I just wasn't good enough at my job, but offered me a job on the party committee.

My first job on the party committee? Cleaning the bar's bathrooms and keeping them tidy all evening.

I am not above any job. I clean my own bathrooms at home and even cleaned for my grandpa as a job once. But I was 20 years old with half of a college degree and several years of job experience…was that really the only job the bar could offer me?

I don't think so.

Around this time my grandpa started to be sick and was in the hospital. My mom needed me more than I needed the money from the bar. So I quit my job, promising I would come back and work for them someday and I was free to head back to Bloomington.

...and the torture continues: Junior Year

In the fall of 2010, my parents and I caravanned down to Bloomington, one blue Ford SUV after another, the entire four hours to my new apartment. We unpacked the car, unpacked the storage unit I had rented, and we crammed it all into my apartment. After my mom and I had been organizing and unpacking for hours, I sat back and began to cry.

"I just want it to look nice," I sobbed, while staring at the still unfinished mess, "That's all I want."

Clearly, I wasn't going to be any less dramatic as a junior.

But two Target trips, numerous hours, and a few beers later, my single apartment was decked out and ready for me. Before decoration, it looked depressing and tiny. But after my mom's amazing decorative touch however, the place was glorious.

I had a half-kitchen which led into my living room. My dad had sanded down and painted an old microwave stand black and stacked two black wooden boxes on either side of it. The two pieces together looked like an entertainment center complete with my sleek (and cheap) silver TV and DVD's stacked around it. Above the TV was a piece of wood that I had painted pink and secured some black and white photos I had taken to it. The photos were of things in the world that looked like the letters in my name and was a very cool addition to my "grown up" place. My couch was a cheap futon bought at a church garage sale with zebra striped and pink assorted throw pillows that my mom had made for me. My dad had fashioned a coat-rack for me out of a post and some street signs that my mom had gotten me for my 19th birthday, and my brother had bought me a beautiful kitchen table and stools. My bedroom looked similar to the room that I had with my cheerleader roommates, complete with pink bedding, a desk, and my signature "bottle cap" coffee table. My dad made this particular table after my freshman year and it was my favorite piece of furniture. The small table had space for hundreds of beer bottle caps which I arranged into different designs whenever the mood struck me. A sheet of Plexiglas lay over the top of the bottle tops to ensure they did not move, and when I flipped a switch, a set of lights inside the glass lit up.

How COOL is my dad?

I was all set in my new place and ready to be independent and seriously single.

How many times am I going to say the words "seriously single" in reference to myself in college?

I spent my first night in the apartment nervous about my new surroundings. It was strange going from living in a house with my family, to living in a dorm with hundreds of other students, to living with three other girls, to finally living alone. It was oddly comfortable though. I could watch television in the living room without disturbing someone else, do the dishes whenever and however I wanted to, and my fridge was always as full as I had left it. Things in my seriously single apartment were seriously great.

The second evening I was there I had a special guest. I had tried to keep up my friendship with Jacob since things had kind of broken off. While I am starting to realize NOW (in my more adult years) that befriending boys is nearly impossible for me, back then I thought it was an endearing quality that only I possessed. So on the second evening of my stay in Bloomington, Jacob came over to visit. Apparently, his room at the house was piled full of boxes from his other fraternity brothers moving in and out of their respective rooms. So to escape the madness, he sought peace and quiet in my apartment. I had made things very clear before he came over; we were just friends. We may have flirted a lot over the years, but I was not going to get mixed up in the world of Jacob again.

Oh, who was I kidding?

So my "friend" came over. We watched movies off my laptop (very small), we cuddled a little (due to his smooth talking), and eventually I felt comfortable. We could be friends who just hung out, snuggled, watched movies…

And occasionally made out.

Oops.

Jacob was (in my mind at least) labeled a "casual guy." We would never be serious, he never wanted to be serious, and I just had to make my peace with that. I managed to silence the voice that told me, "You are not a casual girl," and convinced myself I could go with the flow.

Sounds like a recipe for a hilarious disaster.

In reality, I need consistency. I need someone to be there for me no matter what, NOT someone who invites me to a party so I could see him there with someone else.

Ugh.

Jacob aside, this year was going to be different. I was going to stop "recycling" boys (you know...AFTER Jacob), start being a responsible student, and I was going to get a job.

Hello job applications, goodbye sanity.

I went to the local radio station, to different tanning salons and retail shops, and finally to an exercise studio in a strip mall in town.

I had never set out to apply there, but it was on the way to Jimmy John's from the tanning salon and they (fatefully enough) were looking for someone to work on Tuesdays and Thursdays. I handed in an application, not expecting to get a job there at all – until they called me for an interview.

Thank God.

The night before the interview I panicked and prayed like it was my job (no pun intended). In the middle of my panic, Jacob's ex-girlfriend Katie texted me, asking me if I had been talking to Jacob about her lately.

Oops.

Katie, upon the end of her relationship with Jacob, began to befriend me for some weird reason. We had talked a little bit here and there, but mostly I was confused as to why she wanted to talk to me. I didn't have anything to do with their relationship, nor did I ever stand in the way of it, and she and I hadn't hung out much. But she was really nice and apparently in need of some girl talk, so who was I to be mean to her? In this budding relationship with my ex-fling's ex-girlfriend, however, I did not realize that my loyalties were to be explicitly to her and I was to dump Jacob as a friend.

My life is so complicated.

So when Jacob and I had our visit, I confided in him that I was a bit uncomfortable with Katie's current kinship with me and asked him about it. That was pretty much the extent of our conversation about her. I knew she was upset about their break up, I knew he was in a weird place with the whole thing, and I knew I wanted to stay out of it.

Easy enough.

But she soon found out that we had talked, and was now texting both he and I about the situation. Well, that was all that I needed that evening. I was stressed about this interview, I was worried about my junior year, and now this girl was starting up drama? Not okay at all.

"I guess I didn't realize that you and Jacob were such good friends after all of this," she texted, obviously pissed.

"Sorry I didn't tell you?" I texted back with a twinge of annoyance. Why was this suddenly my fault?

"We were friends. Why did you have to tell him everything? You don't tell me everything about him. It's just a little rude that you acted all mad at him when really you were still friends with him," she rambled...on and on.

"So I guess if you didn't want to know everything I shouldn't tell you how great of a kisser he still is," I sassed back.

When did I become such a bitch?

The truth of the matter is that I looked at the way Jacob saw me and didn't like it. He saw me as the same little girl I was freshman year, thanking the sober fraternity driver and not knowing what a Long Island Iced Tea was. And I even saw that freshman girl...the one who couldn't stand up to her roommate when she wanted to, or the one who was stuck under her RA's giant thumb. I couldn't help but worry if I was still that girl, and if I had changed even a little from my freshman year to my junior year. My bitchy moment was a test to myself, to see if I could stand up for myself and take care of myself more than I could have as a freshman.

I passed with flying colors.

I still cannot believe I said what I did to that poor girl.

Whatever she texted back to me, I completely ignored. I turned off my phone and computer and went to bed, ready to wake up the next day and get interviewed.

Now I was a force to be reckoned with.

I woke up early, showered, shaved my legs, and blow dried my hair straight. I wore faux diamond studs in my earlobes and pulled my hair into a tight ponytail. I slid into my black "business" dress that had a pencil skirt, slid on my black pumps, and headed to my interview at the exercise studio.

Yes, I was a little overdressed. But I did not care. If college had taught me anything at all, first impressions can be lasting impressions. I walked into the studio and sat down to wait for my interviewer, saying a silent prayer that the job would be mine.

In truth, I was perfect for the position. The establishment was an aerobic, or "Zumba," place. My job was to check in customers, take their money, and occasionally sell workout wear that was on display in the studio. With my dance experience, my workout history, and my past work experience in the dance boutique, I had everything it took to work for ZumDance Studio.

Apparently, they thought so too, and they hired me.

And we were in business, indeed.

Lesson Number 28: How NOT to road trip with frat boys

The first weekend that I had the job, I had already committed to going to South Bend, Indiana to visit my cousin Alyssa at Notre Dame. Alyssa is from Austin, Texas originally, but she is one of my extended family members that I feel the closest to. Alyssa and I first met when I was about 7 years old at a family reunion in downtown Chicago. We instantly clicked, and soon I was visiting her and her sister Kate on a biannual basis. With Alyssa so close at Notre Dame, it was silly for me not to go up to see her. Again, my dear friend Jacob came to the rescue, as he was heading up to South Bend to go to a Notre Dame football game and visit family. After some heavy hinting, he offered me a ride up there.

Lucky, LUCKY Brittney...

So I embarked on an adventure to Notre Dame. I was told we were leaving at noon, so I trekked over to Jacob's house with my bag full of clothes about ten minutes early so I would not get made fun of for being late.

The boys were still sleeping.

I waited. And, for the record, I had dehydrated myself all day for this. Guys are notorious for hating when girls stop them on their road trips to go to the bathroom, and I knew it would be a car full of "he-man-woman-haters."

We left at four in the afternoon.

Let the record also show that I did not know we were leaving, and did not know we would be leaving four hours after the time I was told.

Of course, even after all my rigorous bladder training, two and a half hours into the trip I had to pee. It is not that I didn't hold it, I did. For a whole painful 45 minutes I held it, before I asked Jacob if we could stop.

His response? "No."

So not funny.

In general, I drive myself almost everywhere. If I am not driving, Hannah or my dad is. I have rarely been in a situation where I was not permitted to stop whenever I wanted to. Needless to say, I was going nuts. I kept moving around. I kept shifting in my seat. It started in my palms, but slowly my entire body was sweating. I needed to go and NOW. I was in physical pain.

After finally stopping to let me pee (thank you, Jacob) I spent the rest of the car ride learning "how to be the perfect woman." It was the funniest hour of my life. From learning about fantasy football, to learning about different cars and how to make them faster, the guys tried to educate me as much as they could in the ways of "their kind."

I had so much fun on my "guy ride" to Notre Dame, but I was relieved to meet up with my cousin at the end of the journey. I was craving some serious girl time.

Alyssa and I always have fun together. She had the weekend packed full of fun stuff, and I got to meet all of her friends. I wore green to the Notre Dame vs. Purdue game, and cheered Notre Dame on to victory! I even caught a glimpse of Taylor Swift (who was at the game with her brother, a Notre Dame student), and possibly Selena Gomez. Needless to say, it was an amazing weekend.

Unfortunately, I had to leave the magical, mystical land that was Notre Dame and head back to Bloomington (with an empty bladder this time) to go to school and my new job at ZumDance. My boss had called to ask me if I wouldn't mind working on Fridays, in addition to my Tuesday and Thursday obligations.

"No problem," I had responded, "Anything you want."

As my life goes, I headed into my first day of training with strep throat. I was as sick as a dog, but I held my head high and worked as hard as I could. I was led around the studio, taught how to work everything, and was told a few simple rules:

Make sure the place stays clean;

Make sure the customers feel welcomed; and,

As long as 1 and 2 are taken care of, feel free to do homework.

Oh yeah...I could get used to this.

Lesson Number 29: How to get in over your head (or, learning the underrated art of saying "no")

After a week of working at ZumDance, I was asked to work on Sundays too. I was a little hesitant. I had signed up for Tuesdays and Thursdays, was added on to Fridays, and now I was working all day Sunday? Suddenly, my 10 to 15 hour a week job had become a 23 to 27 hour a week job. I was worried my grades would slip and that I'd become overwhelmed once Hoosierettes practice began, but I felt as if I could not say no. I took the hours and remained silent, figuring I could always cut back if I needed to.

A few weeks later, Hoosierettes practice began. Leading a team was going to be harder than I had imagined. I had figured that the hardest part was going to be getting girls to show up. But suddenly there were 12 of them there, staring at me, expecting me to dance, and I hadn't really planned that far.

Oops.

To my credit, I had done an amazing job starting up the team. I had had schedules made up, I had organized uniforms, and I had even typed up several rules and policies to ensure that the team would run smoothly.

What I didn't really plan on was everyone having their own opinion about how the team should go from there.

For starters, half of the girls hated the uniforms and half of the girls loved them. I had gone through a ton of trouble to get them sent to me so the girls could try them on, and most of the girls did not seem to appreciate the effort, nor the fashions I had chosen. Then, half the uniforms had been backordered – meaning that half of the girls would have to get a different size than they had ordered. This was a mild disaster, but nothing compared to the issues I was having with the Athletic Department.

I was assured by a Senior Athletic Director in the previous year that my ideas were bringing up student involvement in a positive light, and that I would be able to discuss the issue further in the following year. What the department left out was that they weren't really going to talk to me the following year. I received little to no feedback from emails and letters that I sent to the department, and I was growing increasingly upset. I had twelve girls expecting department validation, and no contact with the said department.

Crap.

Finally, after weeks of emails, the Hoosierettes got our "big break," and were invited to perform at halftime at a women's basketball game. Not only was I excited, but the girls were. We choreographed a dance, rehearsed hard, and even scheduled more practices to make it happen. I emailed the woman who scheduled our performance to ask what time we should arrive and who we should give our music to.

We received no response.

The night before the performance, the Athletic Department emailed me, telling me that our performance was no longer needed at that game. After all the work the team and I had put in, we had been rejected.

What the Athletic Department didn't count on was that I was not going to back down so quickly.

While the situation that the Hoosierettes were in sucked, my job sucked more. I had met some amazing people, but the management team at the company sucked – and everybody knows that bad management in a company spells disaster.

And what a disaster it was.

One of my managers was an 18 year old who was a friend of the owner's family. I had a girl who was two years younger than me and in community college telling me what to do on a daily basis. Wasn't I too young to have a boss that was younger than me? I know that as you get older that becomes a greater possibility, but I was freshly 20 years old. It seemed a little strange to me that an 18 year old was my superior. My other manager was just as confused as the owner about to how to employ college students and how to run a business.

Seems like a solid foundation for failure.

Toward the end of October, the studio's stereo system began to break completely. The instructors and I watched it spark and flame, smoke, or just completely turn off during our shifts. This studio's classes were nothing without music. With each malfunction, I began to run home and get the stereo I used for Hoosierette practices. The stereo was made for iPods and was a Christmas gift from my parents. At first, I didn't mind lending it to the studio when I could, so I spent my evenings running back and forth to my apartment or my car to grab it and keep the classes going. I was bending over backwards for these people, and my effort was always met with, "Can you bring it over again today?" and "Why can't we have it all evening?"

One particular night at work, I was asked to bring in the stereo for the 6:30 A.M. Zumba class. I am not much of a morning person (I schedule all classes after 10:00 A.M.). But for the good of the company, I woke my ass up, wearily pulled on yoga pants and a tee, and dragged myself to the studio. Not only did I wake up early, but 6:15, 6:30, and then 6:45 rolled by and nobody showed up, including the instructor. I called my dad in a rage, telling him that I could not believe what had happened and that I was still working for them. But, I needed the money, and I wasn't going to be in the financial situation to quit anytime soon.

So I complained quietly and continued to work, even though I hated the establishment. I hated the moldy mop I had to use to wash the floors, I hated the vacuum that I used to clean up the dirt tracked in by customers, and I hated the patronizing tone the owner used when she talked to me. Why was I bending over backwards for these people?

I hadn't taken off a day of work yet, but I took a day off for the Hoosierettes performance in the Homecoming Parade. This was not only because I was performing with the team, but also because that special someone was coming back into town.

That's right...Lizzie was coming!

Lizzie had come to help me with the Homecoming Parade, to aid in the smooth functioning of the Hoosierettes dinner with the fraternity after, and to live it up and party with me after it was all over.

My weekend off was going to be a weekend to remember, indeed.

Unfortunately, my boss called a "mandatory work meeting" the Sunday after Homecoming at 10:00 A.M. I wouldn't party too much anyway, so I figured I would be able to make it.

Piece of cake...right?

The Homecoming Parade went very well. Because of the cancellations that the Athletic Department had made, it was the Hoosierettes first official performance. The girls shone so bright and our smiles were from ear to ear as we marched the team through campus. The dinner at the fraternity was wonderful. But Saturday night, after the excitement of the football game was over, was when my weekend really began.

And ended.

Lesson Number 30: How to make an ass out of yourself (over and over again)

When Lizzie comes to visit, I am singularly determined to show her a good time. Since the last time she had visited was pretty dramatic, I had decided that I was going to be on my best behavior.

Or maybe my worst.

Lizzie and I began the evening by dressing up, dancing around my apartment, and…taking shots. As a gift to me, Lizzie brought two double shot glasses decorated with pink zebra stripes. Since we couldn't really tell where the single shot line was, I was free-pouring. My brother had stashed some quality vodka in my suitcase at the beginning of the year and with Lizzie there, I finally had a reason to open it up. Several shots in we both confessed that we "didn't really feel it yet" and kept drinking.

My best and worst stories begin this way.

We continued drinking, and then walked over to the fraternity with a big glass of water. At the time, I was convinced that the giant glass of water was going to stop my current nausea.

Well, it was a nice try.

We arrived at the party and things were already started. The music was pounding, girls in tiny skirts and high heels were crowding around the door, and the drinks were pouring. Lizzie and I had teased and sprayed our hair, put sparkly eye shadow along our eyelids – and, with a double coat of mascara, we each looked a few years older than we actually were. We both wore strappy tops and cute shoes and were at our personal best.

Except for the fact that the pair of us were too drunk to hold a coherent conversation.

The coolest thing about that fraternity was that they all knew Lizzie and I quite well. We got pushed to the front of the line to get in, carried over to the bar when our drinks were empty, and were never without a single thing that we wanted. It was the college equivalent of being a celebrity and on the VIP list, and I loved every moment of it.

Lizzie and I signed up for beer pong…oh my goodness was that a mess. Neither of us was seeing straight, I could barely stand up, and Lizzie kept leaving the table and coming back.

"Where does she keep going off to?" I wondered, mainly to myself.

But instead of investigating, I kept drinking determined to "keep up the buzz."

Buzz is defined by Urban Dictionary as "the feeling of being inebriated from alcohol or any mind-altering substance." Drunk is described (again by Urban Dictionary) as "when you have to hold on to the grass to keep from falling off the earth." If it's possible, I was far beyond both of those definitions.

Lizzie, as it turns out, kept leaving the pong table to vomit up the booze I had given her. Once some fraternity boy or another had pointed that out, I spent some quality bonding time with her while holding her hair back. We were such a good team. I have memories of her telling me that I "should go get a boy tonight," and that I was, "so pretty." I should have known that we were both in trouble then.

Jacob laughed as we both walked around; me stumbling and Lizzie strutting in her "drunk strut" as we like to call it. I flirted with everyone, and eventually blacked out. At the time, everything was funny and a good time.

It wasn't nearly as funny when we got home.

I was not in good shape. Now I was vomiting, Lizzie was holding MY hair back, and I have no memory of any of it...but the mess I left behind was proof. When I woke up at 7:00 A.M. the next morning, I was convinced that I had lost my phone, I was still wearing my denim skirt and black tank top, and my pillows were streaked with black makeup.

Classy.

What I wouldn't remember until later was that in this state of pure misery, I would have to go to my "mandatory staff meeting" at ZumDance.

Crap.

I dragged myself to the car ten minutes before the meeting was to begin, drove over to the studio, and plopped myself down in a seat.

Yeah, this was going to be fun.

I sipped a grape sports drink as the meeting went on, nursing my uneasy stomach. I got to hear about how business was not doing well, about how we all needed to work hard on getting more members at the studio, and how about how we were all responsible for that (all while fighting the urge to vomit in my purse). The owner's mother was talking mainly to the instructors at this point, and I couldn't figure out why the hell I was there. The only thing that was directed toward me was a lecture on professionalism – something I had always been an expert at. After two hours of pure hell, we were finally dismissed.

Exactly 2 hours and 20 minutes after the meeting began, I threw up.

I had never been that hungover in my entire life, and I never plan to be again. I had, however, shown my dedication to the job by showing up no matter what. Since I had claimed I was just sick and not hungover at that meeting, I figured that my job was still secure as I put in for the shifts I wanted in the following semester.

I had figured wrong.

After the meeting, I began getting really rude text messages from the owner and manager. It wasn't like they hadn't seen me all evening. No, they would talk with me (often pleasantly), leave the job site, and text me mean things when they got in the car.

"Stop sitting on your ass and actually do something today."

"Why haven't our numbers gone up? What are you doing wrong? You're failing us."

This is what covered my text inbox as they used my stereo, as I worked almost all the shifts, and as I really wanted the business to succeed.

I really hated them.

It was at this time that I was asked to compose a list of sorority presidents for the company to use to contact them. ZumDance was going to send an instructor from the studio to the sorority for 40-50 dollars an hour to give the girls a workout class once a week. It seemed like a pretty good idea, so I threw myself into the project with vigor.

A good idea, indeed.

It was a Monday night, my evening off, and I was heading to a dress rehearsal for the Hoosierettes. I had my uniform on, my lipstick all set, and was straightening my bow in my hair as I looked on my computer to my email. There, from the owner of ZumDance, was an email entitled, "Termination Letter..."

What. A. Bitch. She fired me via email!

"Brittany,

I wanted to speak with you tomorrow about the things that I need to see improved but I talked to Sarah R [one of the managers] today and she informed me that she had spoken to you on several accounts about what to/not to do. In fact a couple of people have notified me about your constant facebook use, the shoppers that aren't acknowledge when you work, your dress not being all that professional (when we talked about "dressing" it up for the boutique), not steaming the clothes when instructed to do so and finally not doing the required clean up at the nights end. I feel that ultimately with paying you $8 (which is above minimum wage) that I expect the things that are required of you and done when asked of you.

 I would like to thank you for your time and wish you the best in your future endeavors but your services are no longer needed at this time. By the way make sure I have your correct address you want your check sent to please.

Thanks!"

First of all, the bitch fired me via email, and then she spells my name wrong in my termination letter.

What a brilliant woman I had worked for.

While I will admit I was not the best employee in the entire world, it was a little difficult to be so superior when I was running around trying to get my stereo for them to use, showing up when other people didn't to make sure that the business didn't fail, and so much more! The management in this place stunk, and I was no longer keeping my mouth shut.

Like my old boss, I was turning into an innovative corporate bitch myself.

Lesson Number 31: The opposite of maturity and professionalism

I emailed back:

"I was told when I got the job that I could do whatever I wanted at the front desk as long as the work got done. I was also told that I could wear whatever I wanted to work as long as I looked either Zumba appropriate, or classy looking for the boutique. I was never told that I HAD to dress up. As for customer service, many of the customers have been pleased with my service and I am shocked that you heard that, however, if I may say so, how would you even know of my customer service when you are never at the studio? I did not clean up at the nights end for the past few days because I was a little busy driving to my apartment, running to the dollar store, and buying things for my boom box to fix your business and to save you as a place of business... I have NEVER experienced such unprofessionalism from a business in my entire life. Emails and text messages are NOT the way to run a business at all and you should be ashamed of yourself for firing me over an email. I spent so much of my own money and so much of my own time trying to make this business a success and honestly, if you cannot see that in me then you will fail. Be very careful of the way you are treating your employees because I am not the only one who has been unhappy with the way you and your managers are treating us. I will be in the studio on pay day to receive my check. Don't you worry yourself about that."

Yeah, I still can't believe I did that. Who had I become?

I thought it would be over. She had fired me and I had said all that I needed to say. I thought that we would part ways, I would get my paycheck the following Friday, and this little drama would be over.

Ha.

Five minutes later my cell phone rang, showing her number. *Are you freaking kidding me?* I thought. She basically called in response to my email, to tell me that I was the most disrespectful little girl she had ever met, and that she never liked me much anyways.

"Excuse me, but I just lost my job and you're taking up my daytime minutes," I interrupted her screaming tirade, "Could you please continue this at 9:00 when it is free?"

And then I hung up.

Again, I cannot believe I did that.

Meanwhile, I was panicking. I no longer had a job. I was unemployed and essentially broke. What was I going to do for money?

And then it hit me.

I had that list of sorority presidents' email addresses that I was composing for ZumDance, but never had a chance to turn in. ZumDance was going to charge the sororities about 40-50 dollars for their classes.

Lesson Number 32: How to win.

I sent out emails to every sorority, offering the same classes for 25 dollars per 45 minute session. That semester I had three sorority houses. I was only making 75 dollars per week – and even less when a house cancelled on me – but I was making money while sticking it to the company that had fired me.

ZumDance went out of business that June.

Who has two thumbs, speaks French, and won in that little situation? *Moi.*

It was around the end of October when I was fired from ZumDance, and while I did have an amazing backup plan for a job, I was still bummed. I had never been fired from anything before.

As for my little fling with Jacob, I hadn't been feeling good about it. I am really not meant for flings. As my ex-roommate Hannah once said, "You'd make a fun wife, but not a good casual girlfriend." Deep down, that little voice that had told me I was not a "casual girl" kept surfacing at the worst times. I knew I wasn't the kind of girl that could keep doing this. I decided however, to hide my issues from Jacob. That was the mature thing to do.

Until the night that Maggie, Hannah, and I went to the psychic.

We didn't set out to go to a psychic. Hannah had wanted to get her "industrial" piercing, and somehow had talked me into getting my cartilage pierced. I had wanted the piercing for a while, and had even gotten it in high school – until my mom had threatened to not pay for college if I did not take it out. The opportunity was too good to pass up; so, both happily pierced, we paid and left the tattoo parlor, and I spent a year hiding my new piercing from my parents.

Down the road from the tattoo parlor was the psychic's home and business. I had never believed in psychics, but Maggie thought it was going to be fun, and since I was not going to pay for any services I figured I could go and watch. When the psychic read Maggie's palms, she was oddly accurate about Maggie's past and her fears. But what struck me most about her was when she turned and looked at me after Maggie's palm reading was done.

"You," she said pointing to me, "You're trying to be someone different for a boy. Stay true to yourself and if he leaves because of it...let him. You'll find the right one by being yourself."

And that advice she offered to me for free.

That was the end of Jacob, for good this time. I had no interest in being toyed with, the psychic was right. So, I aimed to remain friends with him but completely keep romance out of it.

Felt good to have some closure there.

A few days after my psychic experience, I got a phone call from my friend Jacque. Jacque had been Jenny's roommate freshman year, and was a lot of fun. She always had a party to go to, a cute boy on her arm, and was always in on the hottest gossip.

Lesson Number 33: If your life is going too well...add a dash of

drama!

I was sitting in the library (pretending to study, but really just wallowing in self-pity over my current unemployment and lack of romance) when my phone rang. Dodging the stares of the angry studying Asians around me, I answered.

"Hey, it's Jacque," is what I heard on the other end.

Jacque and I had lost touch since freshman year and I wondered why she was calling me.

"Well there's this guy…and wait are you single?" she responded.

After assuring her of my single-ness, she went on to tell me about a cute guy friend of hers that was in desperate need of a good kind girl to talk to, and she had immediately thought of me.

Jacque was great.

The boy in question was a Marine stationed in North Carolina. According to his Facebook, he was tall with brown hair, sparkling brown eyes, and was very muscular. He had an amazing smile and he was really fun to talk to. Jacque said that nothing had to come of it, no pressure, but he needed a friend.

What Jacque did not mention was that the boy – Cole was his name – was currently deployed in Afghanistan.

Oops.

Originally, it didn't really matter. We were just Facebook friends, and spent some time every once in a while chatting. As we rolled into November and then December, however, our attachment to each other became a little more intense.

It isn't really like me to meet someone online, but he was a friend of Jacque's and it was possible I had met him before. He had been friends with Jacque for a while and had visited her before his current deployment, so I used this possibility to justify the relationship in my mind. That Jacque knew him and that he and I may have met before lulled me into a sense of pseudo-security. We got to know each other slowly (is there any other way when the other person is in Afghanistan?), and there seemed no harm in the arrangement.

With him being in a war situation over there, it was hard for him to talk to me every day, but it was also hard for him not to. He needed to reach out to somebody, anybody, over here that would listen to him and would be there no matter what. I figured that that was what I was doing – being a good friend and supporting our troops...or just one troop. He went a little quicker than I did, as falling for me seemed to be in his nature. In his world, he didn't have time to waste trying to go slow. He was honest and true with his feelings because tomorrow he might not be able to talk about it. That is a fact that only women who have loved ones in the military can understand. Time is so precious. Say what you want and say what you mean as soon as possible, before you cannot say it at all.

So I familiarized myself with his situation and his way of living. Every once in a while he would call me or email me saying that that particular day had been difficult and that he was glad that he'd made it through so he could talk to me. We were in our own little world when we talked, whether it was on the phone or online, and it wasn't too long until I started to fall for him too.

A few days before Christmas he told me that he loved me. I had never said that to anyone else before, and I wasn't sure I was ready to say it back. He said he understood, but after a few weeks I had broken down and said it too. I wasn't really sure if I meant it or not, but I wanted to say it in case I never got the chance to. I didn't want any regrets.

Before I knew it, Christmas break was over and I was headed back to Bloomington for school. Breaks always seem to go by so quickly. It's really unfair. But they come and they go, and life moves on.

Oh, who am I kidding? Going back to school sucks. There is no good way to spin that. It was awful and I hated it. But I was floating with my current love (or rather, infatuation) and went back without a fight...this time.

In January, things started to be weird between Cole and me. We had gotten into a discussion about futures and dreams, and he had revealed that he wanted to be a father more than anything in the world, but he still loved being a Marine. I had said that it would take a special woman to want to be a mother to his children while he was away all the time and he told me,

"I thought all women wanted to be stay-at-home moms."

Some girls do (and more power to them) and some girls don't. It may change for me, but I never saw myself as primarily being a mother. When I told him that, he seemed really offended and that's the first time that I realized that Cole might NOT be "the one." It might not work out. In fact, it might not be working out already and he wasn't even back yet.

I am never really good at following my first instincts, so I ignored it.

A few days later, in a phone conversation right before he headed back to North Carolina and finally to the U.S., he revealed that he had been engaged to a girl before. What was even more surprising was the way that he explained the proposal. He blurted it out to the woman to end an argument and remain in a relationship. It seemed more like a desperate need to gain her trust and approval than a declaration of love. He hadn't thought much about it, and eventually the engagement deteriorated, but the story stuck with me like glue.

Something just was not right with this boy.

But he made it back to America in the beginning of February and was going to have a month of "leave," or vacation time, beginning March 1st. Once he got back to North Carolina, he would be able to talk to me more, and under less stress. Things would be easier with him back in the States.

On Valentine's Day, he woke me up to ask me if I wanted him to send me flowers or something. He did things like this on occasion, and those acts continued to reassure me that he was okay and overrule anything bad that he had done that week. I didn't want anything, but I appreciated talking to him and starting my day on the phone with him.

And what a day it would be.

I went to class and felt a little funny, went home and felt a little funny, and spent the evening in bed in pain.

Something was not right.

Hannah called me after she was done working, and I could not contain myself. I began sobbing on the phone, telling her about my pain.

"Okay," she soothed, "Call your Mom and if you need me to, I'll take you to the hospital."

I talked to my mom, and then talked to Lizzie's mom. Lizzie's mom was a nurse at the public school near my house. Since she was concerned it was my appendix, they sent me to the hospital to be checked out.

It was such a hot Valentine's date, sitting in the ER waiting room with Hannah. I wore pink velour sweatpants and a black hoodie. She was wearing jeans and a tee shirt. We were an attractive couple.

I texted Cole to tell him where I was and how I was doing, and I got no response.

Weird.

The doctors did not want to do an MRI, and assumed that I was passing another kidney stone. I was administered medication for the pain and medication for an infection they thought I had and they sent me home.

It was definitely not a kidney stone.

I spent an entire week being unable to eat, and taking the medication but being dizzy and sleepy. I spent every single day being able to digest nothing but Slim Fast shakes (partly because that was the only thing I had) and water. It was awful. I tried calling Cole to talk about it. I figured that since I was there for him in his time of need, he would be there for me too.

He wasn't.

I tried to be understanding, and at the time I really didn't have the energy to think about it too much. I was too busy being sick, too busy being hurt, and too busy wondering when this would all stop.

Five days after my Valentine's Day trip to the emergency room, I woke up to a terrible feeling around 6 A.M. Besides the crimson color that my urine turned the toilet that morning, I could not stand up straight because of the pain I was in, and I didn't know what to do. I called my mom and she sent me to the hospital. She asked if I wanted her to come down to Bloomington, but I said that I would be fine and I would probably be back to my apartment before she even got there.

The issue that I had was that it was, in fact, 6 A.M. and nobody was around to drive me. I thought about calling Hannah or asking my neighbor, but it was just too early to ask anyone and the situation was kind of dire. So I hobbled myself downstairs and waddled to the car. I drove all the way to the hospital crouched over the steering wheel, scared for myself. I was clammy and shaking when I arrived to the Bloomington Emergency Hospital.

I was becoming too frequent a visitor there.

I was near tears when the nurse took my blood pressure and asked me what was wrong. I thought I was going to be sick two different times before the doctor came in and when the nurse came in to administer my IV, I lost it.

It was embarrassing really, throwing such a tantrum at twenty years old. I am not really afraid of needles much, but I am afraid of invasive procedures, and since I had never stayed in the hospital before, this was as invasive as it got for me.

"Please...is this really necessary?" I pleaded with the male nurse in charge.

"Yes," he responded.

Clearly, he did not have a great bedside manner.

"Listen...I think I am going to vomit. That is how scared of this IV thing I am...please don't make me do this," I cried.

"Please hold still," he responded.

Great.

The second they put that IV in me, I called my mom and told her I needed her to get down there. I had no idea what the rest of the day would entail, but this was going neither as quickly nor as smoothly as I thought it would.

The IV ended up not being too bad though. Whatever awesome pain medication they put in there got me nice and loopy.

"Hey!" I nearly yelled as they rolled me down to my MRI, "How cool is this? My bed is MOVING."

I'd say that IV was not the worst thing that had ever happened to me.

Of course, before the meds kicked in, I had texted Hannah and begged HER to come stay with me too, so by the time I was done with my MRI, Hannah had come to see me.

"Hey Hoppy," I said. "I know her. That's my friend!" I told the nurse.

Gotta love that IV.

The doctor came back in to tell me that I had a burst ovarian cyst, and that I was going to be fine, but to control my pain he was going to write me a prescription for hydrocodone. What I didn't realize at the time was that hydrocodone was fancy "doctor talk" for what is commonly referred to as Vicodin.

Rock ON.

Lesson Number 34: When all else fails, prescriptions and Mommy are good alternatives

I walked outside with Hannah and was immediately perplexed by all of the colors in the world.

We were in a cement parking garage.

Hannah thought this whole thing was hilarious as she dropped me off at my apartment. Because of the fabulous medication I was on, I was not permitted to drive and needed to pick up my car at a later time. My mom showed up an hour or so later (after I frantically ran through my apartment and cleaned it), and we got my prescriptions.

College students understand that when you're sick in college, nobody takes care of you. You get your own Sprite when your tummy aches, you get your own soup when you have a cold, and you administer your own medication as needed. But my mom was staying the night at my house to make sure I was going to be okay. I went to take a nap and woke up to homemade chicken noodle soup. I went to bed that night and woke up to clean windows and a clean kitchen. The next day, since I had also had a cold at the time, she took me to breakfast and then to the Laundromat where we washed every single soft surface including my bedding, towels, and clothes. We spent three hours and forty dollars in quarters, but we got it all done, clean, and put the apartment back together.

My mom is truly amazing.

Through all of this, Cole never asked how I was feeling. In fact, it was then that I decided I would not talk to him until he tried to call me again.

That would teach him.

But he did call that Monday to say that he was sorry he was so busy and to ask how I was feeling.

Smooth. Very smooth indeed.

February also brought the Hoosierettes' first performance on the road in a town near Louisville, Kentucky. We did a great job, and the excitement of performing definitely had me and the other girls ready and excited to work harder the following year.

But surprisingly, February's performance was just a flicker on my radar – what I was really looking forward to was March and the arrival of Cole.

March 1st, Cole left North Carolina and headed straight to Bloomington to see me. He arrived at about 7:00 P.M., and I thought I was going to die of excitement. I ran down the stairs of the apartment complex and watched as he stepped out of the car.

He was every bit as beautiful as Jacque and Facebook depicted him. He was so tall, but it didn't seem to matter as I jumped up to give him a hug and a kiss. I'll never forget the look on his face as he saw me for the first time; he looked so happy and excited like "finally, she's here." It was perfect, and on that day I was convinced that he himself was perfect.

I had set up my apartment with all of my Christmas, Thanksgiving, Valentine's Day, and Halloween decorations, so that he and I could celebrate all of the holidays he had missed on his deployment. I pulled out movies like "Hocus Pocus," "Valentine's Day," and "Elf" to continue the celebration. We each had a drink and sat back to watch a movie, but mostly we kissed. It was the perfect evening.

Later we went to Denny's for food. I had been sick but I ordered a stack of pancakes and a Dr. Pepper. He ordered an orange juice and switched our drinks. He wanted me to get some vitamin C and be healthy for his time in Indiana.

Oh. My. God. So. Adorable.

He paid for food, he opened doors, and he even picked me up and spun me around sometimes. He was perfect, and I was as close to love as I ever thought I could be. When he dropped me off at my apartment, I found that he had left his military dog tags for me to wear on my coffee table. When I asked him about it, he said that he wanted me to have them, and that he was excited to see me that following Saturday.

If I had to put money on it, I'd bet I was more excited than he was.

The next few days I could not stop gushing about how much I loved him. He was great to me and I was in love with him…what could go wrong?

The day he was supposed to come visit, I was at Hannah's doing laundry.

"Hey babe! I am at Hannah's doing laundry. She'll bring me home at 4 or you can come get me then when you come into town!" I texted him, since I figured he was on his way.

At 4:30, a half an hour after he was supposed to be there, he texted saying he was not going to make it.

Weird.

He texted me later to tell me that he was sick and that he was sorry. He would be there at 9:00 the next morning without question, and we would spend the entire day together.

Or so he promised.

At the same time, my brother was going to be in Bloomington at 8 A.M. to load up my broken car onto a trailer to be fixed back at home.

Great. My Marine love interest was going to get to meet my ex-Navy brother.

I woke up that day at 7:00 A.M. to shower and get ready. I never, ever get up that early on a weekend. I sat on the couch to watch early morning television and waited. Eight o'clock rolled around, and my brother had not arrived. At 8:30 and he still wasn't there, and was not answering his phone. At 9:00, neither Cole nor my brother John had showed up.

I was being doubly stood up.

My brother eventually called me back to say that he was going to show up at noon, and Cole called shortly before John arrived and told me that, again, he was not going to make it.

"I am just so sick hun. I promise I will be there tomorrow. We can have dinner I swear," he said to me that day.

Fine, he would get one more chance.

With John taking my car back home to Chicago for a new transmission, I was stuck without transportation. So, the next morning when I woke up with a sore throat and white pus on my tonsils, I panicked. Hannah was out of town and I had no way to get my throat assessed.

My first instinct was to call Cole and ask him to come get me. He said that he would leave as soon as he could but he would be tied up for a bit. So I arranged for Jenny and Hannah to take me to the "PromptCare" health clinic, and counted on Cole to be able to drive me home.

Well...it was a good plan until Cole decided that he did not want to get sick, so he would not be coming to get me.

Bastard.

Hannah, my non-romantic life partner, drove from Anderson, Indiana to the clinic to pick me up, take me to CVS to get my prescription filled, get me some juice, and take me home.

How many times in college can one girl say her best friend is amazing? Because I don't think I can say it enough...yep...wait...here it comes...

She rocks.

I got home, however, to an empty apartment, sick AGAIN, with no boy to confide in.

Again, I wondered if maybe Cole was not right for me after all.

The following Monday, he called to apologize for his indecency and plan his arrival for that Tuesday night. He knew I had class until 8:00, but promised he would be there shortly after that and we could spend the night and the entire day Wednesday together.

When would I stop believing him?

I disinfected my entire apartment. I scrubbed everything with anti-bacterial wipes, soaked my dishes in boiling hot water and soap, and washed all of my sheets and towels. A germ could not survive in that sterile environment if it tried. I was ready for his arrival.

Which never came.

I know I should have seen it coming...but I never expected someone to treat me like that. I am a big fan of the Golden Rule and I would never treat someone the way that Cole treated me. I called him seven times. I texted him five times. I called my mom and Lizzie, crying hysterically to both, wondering where he was and if he was going to be okay. Was he in a car wreck? Was he in the hospital? What was going on?

I slept with my phone in my hand, desperate to get a call from him. But that call never came. The next morning I was a hot mess. I faked enthusiasm through a business call about a choreography job for a high school dance team (which I got!), but other than that, I could not handle the day. When Hannah arrived with Starbucks, I melted in her arms and cried. I turned off my phone to get some homework done. I still had a life to live. His voicemail to me during that time was a little strange.

"I don't want to...um...talk...A friend of mine...its nothing....You wouldn't understand...Bye."

None of his ramblings made sense. I texted him a bunch of times after that, until he responded, saying that he was having a rough time because a friend of his had passed away on deployment overseas. He was upset and didn't want to see or talk to anyone. I guess I could understand that (although at this point my patience was running thin), and I told him to get back to me when he could or he could even come visit me in Chicago. He seemed to love the idea of seeing me in my hometown, and told me he would make plans to do so. He said he loved me and we would talk when the bad stuff was over.

A few hours later, around 1:00 AM, Hannah called me.

"Hey," I said a little tentatively. Usually, Hannah did not call me that late unless something was terribly wrong.

"Hi. Have you checked Facebook today?" she responded.

Apparently, I had somehow missed the photos of Cole – dated the days he was "sick" – at a party. He was kissing another girl, he had a hickey, and it suddenly sank in that I had been played. I tried to rationalize. I thought that maybe they were just old photos that had been recently uploaded, but the watermark left by the camera did not lie.

I had been played. There was no tragic death of a Marine left behind in Afghanistan. Or, maybe there was. Either way that was not why he had not been around to see me. He was busy in other ways.

I was outraged. I had no idea why he did that to me. And not only did he do that to me, he did it with a girl who had no eyebrows (talk about "over-waxing" – she looked perpetually surprised...easy with the tweezers, man-stealer). I was trying to be "Christian" and not dwell on it...but that never works on a woman scorned. So, I did the unthinkable and called my house while my parents were sleeping.

"I'd like to chop off his balls and feed them to him," my mom said at one point during that conversation.

She is amazing.

Hannah and Lizzie were hilarious in helping me deal with the situation. Lizzie commented on Facebook that he would never escape hers and Hannah's "ginger power bitchessss" (as both girls have red hair), while Hannah cursed him saying, "May the fleas of a thousand camels infest the crotch of any Marine who breaks your heart and may his arms be too short to scratch."

My friends are awesome.

I was pretty depressed. This was the second guy in college who had walked out on me without giving a reason. In a moment of pathetic desperation, I found my old flame Michael's Facebook and sent him a message asking if he wanted to talk sometime soon. His response?

"I'm so glad you messaged me, I got a new phone and don't have your number. I'm doing… eh alright and I would love to talk to you again. Hope you're doing well and hope to talk to you soon."

I sent him my number, he sent me a text, and we spent the rest of the night (until 7 A.M.) talking on the phone or texting. Even though I knew romantic involvement was out of the question (fool me once…), it was nice to hear from an old friend and talk about where things had gone wrong. Basically, we had both been immature, and that's why we stopped talking.

Michael was amazing. He helped me get through the next few days so much. When Cole called to apologize and ask if I could forget everything that had happened, Michael kept me in perspective. When I saw more of Cole with his girlfriend on Facebook, Michael comforted me and told me jokes. I was so lucky to have him.

I was still depressed over the whole "Cole Situation," but things were looking up for me because my mom had signed me up for bartending school over spring break. With my wounds healing, I headed back to Chicago ready to get a fresh start and work on a new hobby of mine.

Bartending school was a blast. I learned how to make so many drinks, learned different grades of liquor, and learned how to free pour shots without measuring. It kept my mind off my current heartbreak, and really taught me a valuable skill.

Sadly, my alcoholic dream was dashed when randomly, in the middle of the week, Cole sent me a text saying that he was sorry about what he had done to me. He was trying to "make it right" and he hoped that I would not be so hurt by my experience with him that I would not be able to fall in love again.

What a cocky asshole.

Of course, in a Michael-less moment of weakness, I told Cole that I didn't understand why he was doing these things to me and why things had to be this way.

He stopped responding.

Later that day I figured out why.

As I did every day, I got home from bartending school and went straight onto my computer to check my Facebook. When I got online, I noticed that I had a message in my inbox and I opened it up. It was from the girl in the photos with Cole, and she just wanted to ask if anything was still going on between the two of us. She did not want to get played, nor did she want me to, and she seemed really nice and sensible.

Great, I thought, *this girl can finally know what's really going on. Awesome.*

So I told her that he had told me that he loved me on the phone earlier that week, that he had tried to get me back, and that he had even left me his dog tags from when he was in the war. I told her that she was a grown up and that she could make her own decisions, but that he was a tricky man and to be careful. I thought that this was a friendly conversation and that she was asking out of pure curiosity.

I am never right.

She fired back a message saying that I was a liar, that she had seen the emails and text messages he sent breaking up with me (which I sure never saw and to this day have never received), and that she never wanted to hear from me again.

Excuse me, bitch, but YOU were the one who contacted ME.

Shaking with anger, I sent him a text and told him that I did not want to hear from him again, nor did I want to hear from her. I told him that if she kept finding ways to message me after I had blocked her, he and I were going to have serious issues.

It was an empty threat – I don't have the guts to do that to anyone, no matter how terrible they were to me.

My empty threat, however, was effective because after that day I did not hear from him or her (at least directly) ever again.

In the middle of my senior year, a mutual friend of ours told me that the two of them had gotten married.

"Great. Now they can go ahead and make tan, eyebrow-less, dumbass babies," Hannah said when I told her.

Clearly, we weren't still too bitter about it.

At the end of spring break that junior-year-from-hell, I had managed to graduate from bartending school, suppress some of my health issues, and graduate from "The Cole Era."

The best thing that happened in that situation was that I found my way back to Michael. No matter what awkward things happened between us romantically, we always took care of each other when we needed it. For the rest of that semester, I had someone else to lean on. He drove to Bloomington more times that he needed to, just to check on me or spend time with me, and it really felt good to be friends again.

Little 500 Week rolled around again, and this year I was determined to make the week less of a failure. The schedule of events was full of fun, and my friends and I deserved it. With the year I was having, I felt that I could use a week full of parties and relaxation.

On Monday, Hannah and her roommate James hosted a "Clique" party at their apartment. The instructions were to dress like a high school clique member, whether it was a jock, a rebel, a prep, etc. Because in high school I was a strict rule follower, I decided to be rebellious – wearing my high school uniform with torn up fishnets, terrible shoes, dark makeup, excessive jewelry, and the worst offense yet: leaving my shirt un-tucked. As far as Catholic school kids go, I was the biggest rebel there was.

Or at least, I thought so.

For Little 500 Week and Little 500 Week alone, I had saved up some money and bought myself a fifth of Skyy vodka. As far as college town drinking, it was the highest grade of liquor any of us had bought. I had planned on the bottle lasting me the entire week of celebrations. I left it in Hannah's freezer when she took me home at the Clique Party's end, and I figured it would remain safe.

Unattended booze in a college town? What was I thinking?

The next day I had planned on writing a paper and bypassing the festivities, as a big, expensive concert was happening in Assembly Hall. I went to my classes, and when I finally fought traffic and made it back to my apartment, I was ready for some intellectual stimulation. I sat down to write, as I have done since the dawn of my college career: with a cup of something caffeinated (usually a Diet Coke) and some sort of forensic television show in the background.

Yes, we were in business.

The sun was setting through the windows behind me and the apartment had this romantic glow. Of course, I noticed all of this because instead of writing about Jesus for a Religious Studies course I was taking, I was busy doing everything but my homework. I guess I was so busy procrastinating I did not even notice my phone ring. When I finally got to it, I had a voicemail.

"Hey Brittney, call me back."

Thanks for the context as to who this was.

I texted the number and found out it was our friend Leah, who was with Hannah at the concert. As it turned out, Hannah was desperately needed to get home, since she had had too much to drink at the bar before the concert.

I have no problem being there for Hannah when she needs me. I really don't. She has done so much for me. The only issue, however, was that she was at the basketball arena seeing a very popular rap artist and that traffic there was outrageous. From my apartment I could see that there was a sea of cars outside the building, and that traffic was being directed away from the parking areas. Even if I could fight my way over there, I would not get into the parking lot without paying.

Leave it to Hannah to make this the most complicated sober ride ever.

I convinced Leah to bring Hannah out of the building toward my apartment complex on 17th Street, but when I got there (twenty minutes later) they weren't there.

"We're near the tennis center!" Leah replied when I called her.

Directing drunk people is a nightmare.

When I finally sweet talked my way into the parking lot and pulled around to where the girls were, Hannah and Leah were talking to a police officer. Even 20 feet away I could tell Hannah was not very coherent and I was worried that the conversation would end badly. But the police officer just needed assurance that she was being picked up and taken home safely. She had some issues getting down the stairs to the car and looked like she was in physical pain as we drove.

"Let's go on a road trip!" Drunk Hannah suggested.

Um. No.

I took her home, where she assured me that she would be fine, and on my way out the door I went to the freezer to grab my icy cold bottle of Skyy vodka.

Which was not there.

I was convinced that someone had taken it. That seemed to be the only solution. Someone at the party the previous night had decided that they wanted it and they took it. I was devastated. I had next to no money and now I had to spend the rest of Little 500 Week sober?

NOT OKAY.

I got home determined to find it. I texted every single one of my friends, asking them if they had taken it by mistake, and texted both Hannah and her roommate James asking them if they knew where it had gone. With no response from anyone, I sunk into a mini-depression and mourned the loss of my fun Little 500 Week.

Until I found out that James had taken it and had drank all of it.

Lesson Number 35: Buy a flask.

He didn't do it on purpose, he thought it was his, but I have to admit I was pretty pissed. I mean, I was unemployed and I had literally saved the same twenty dollar bill for months to buy this nice bottle of booze to drink during that holy week.

I tend to let little things like that ruin my week.

James apologized for his mistake, but nobody has let me live down the day I emailed, Facebooked, and texted every single one of my friends looking for a bottle of booze.

The next day, Wednesday, was the performance of the Hoosierettes at the men's lacrosse game halftime. I personally had never been to a lacrosse game before, but the captain of the team invited us to perform and we were in no position to turn down a performance. Organizing the performance itself, however, was a giant nightmare.

I spent the entire game anxious about when halftime was going to be. There was no clock on the field so there was no way of us to know when we should go on. Oh yeah, and I had never been to a lacrosse game in my life.

Looking back, all of these mild disasters that happened through the first year of the Hoosierettes should have been seen as stepping stones. I should have just used them to learn from them, and not been so hard on myself. It's difficult though, when you start something and want it to succeed so badly. Any kind of disappointment seems like an utter disaster, and any mistake feels like it could be the end of the organization and all of the dreams you had for it.

But as soon as my last performance of my junior year was over, the real excitement began as we drank the rest of the night away in celebration. Those are the moments you remember (or don't) from college. I STILL hadn't finished that Religious Studies paper, so between shots Hannah and James gave me advice on my paper.

Needless to say, I did not do well in that Religious Studies class.

Thursday night of Little 500 Week was also spent in a drunken haze. James had shared some of his Parrot Bay with me to make up for my Skyy loss, and things were looking up.

For the women's bike race, which is held on Friday of Little 500 Week, Hannah had to take a math exam. James and I never spent much time together, just the two of us, but suddenly we found ourselves hanging out and drinking in my apartment, dedicating shots to the silliest things and having a good time.

When we were good and liquored up, we headed straight to the race. We had so much fun laughing and watching the race, even as the weather looked terribly questionable. The fun continued the next day at the men's race with Hannah.

Sometimes, there is a perfect moment in your life where you look around and wish everything could remain like that for just a little bit longer. That weekend was full of them. Sitting in the stands, screaming as the rain beat down on the cinder track, watching the entire university, and seeing the greatest intramural sport that our school offers was just that: perfect.

I had no idea that I would miss those moments so much at the end of the school year.

After my original run-in with the Bloomington Community Hospital that year, I had been feeling sick. On my second run-in with the medical community in Bloomington I was tired and always nauseous. In fact, I had bouts of nausea that would keep me shaking in my bed or on my couch some days, only to be cured with a few hours' time and a glass of water.

Lesson Number 2 Revisited: No expectations = no

disappointments.

Going into the week of my 21st birthday, I felt especially sick and in pain, due to the developing and bursting cysts on my ovaries. People were making a big deal about my 21st, and while I wanted it to be exciting, I knew that I was in no shape to really enjoy it. Lizzie came to visit, and we had big plans for the weekend, but I found myself having difficulty getting into the spirit of the celebration. My parents came down to visit the Saturday before my birthday, along with my aunt and uncle, and we went to lunch, hung out, and took naps in preparation for my big night.

Because Lizzie was not yet 21 and she had driven so far to come for my birthday, I had relocated my party to a local bowling alley where we all could bowl and there would be no ID's required to enter. The party was a lot of fun. I was dressed in a beautiful strapless black dress with my sparkly pink cowboy boots and my giant "21st" tiara for the occasion.

But I was fighting to stay alert.

It was our friend Allison's upcoming birthday as well, so at midnight we wished each other a Happy Birthday and said goodbye as the under 21 year olds headed back to Allison's, and Hannah and I headed to Kilroy's Bar on Kirkwood Ave.

Kilroy's on Kirkwood (also known as Roy's or KOK) was one of Bloomington's landmarks and gives out tee shirts on your birthday. The only reason we were even going, in fact, was to get me my shirt.

On that fateful May 1st, they had run out of shirts.

Without my new shirt, I was bummed. Hannah ordered me a Long Island, but a few sips into it I realized that I just wanted to be home in my bed alone.

Until I got a text from Lizzie.

Oh yeah. Her.

When I went back to get her, she seemed kind of pissed that I had sent her to Allison's and I was becoming pissed that I didn't feel well. Already this was a recipe for disaster. I told her all about my birthday bar experience, and how weird but kind of fun it was, and I kind of thought I saw a flicker of annoyance in her eyes. Maybe we were just tired and grouchy from our series of late nights.

Being a hostess stresses me out, being sick stresses me out, and having to do both in one weekend was too much for me. So when she made some sort of snide comment about having to hear about my bar experience over and over again, I just snapped at her.

Lizzie and I never fight. Our biggest fight that I can remember was over who had better ballet shoes back in the day. So when I asked her why she was pissed at me, why she was being so mean, and why she was even there if she didn't really want to be, it felt like someone else talking.

I really didn't mean to start a fight.

Around 2 A.M., we decided it was a misunderstanding and both went to bed, but under my covers later that night I couldn't shake my anger at everyone. "Stop making a big deal of my birthday! Stop pressuring me to have fun and be a nice hostess!

Leave me alone! Can't you all see I'm not feeling well?" I wanted to yell.

When my parents and Lizzie left the next day, I got to fall asleep on my couch while watching the new Harry Potter DVD I had been given for my birthday. I woke up seven hours later in the evening light to my alarm reminding me that I had dinner plans at Olive Garden. After a giant plate of fettuccini alfredo, I returned home to text Michael and fall back asleep for another hour before he arrived.

Why was I so tired all of the sudden? Was I fighting off a cold or something?

Michael arrived to celebrate my birthday evening. We drank a little in my apartment, watched television, and just snuggled for hours. He is so easy to hang out with. Literally, as long as we have something to watch or something to argue about, we can entertain one another for hours. Neither of us cares about impressing the other, neither of us cares about our personal space or the personal space of the other, and time seemed to fly by.

But I was still tired.

Eventually, leaving me with two birthday cookies and a giant bear hug that only Michael could give, Michael deserted me in the beginning of finals week 2011.

Lesson Number 36: If it can go wrong...it will.

I didn't have many finals, and I knew that the only day I really needed to be feeling good was Thursday, the day I had two finals scheduled one right after the other. I spent the week studying a little, but mostly taking care of myself and trying to feel better. For my birthday, my aunt and uncle had given me some money and I spent some of my finals week looking on Craigslist for a new futon, since my old one was very broken.

I found a beautiful leather futon that was nearby in Bloomington, and I called my mom to ask what she thought. It was clear that the couch would not be around much longer, it was a good deal and it was in good condition. So, I made an appointment to go see it on Thursday morning before I went to my finals.

It's funny how I did this to myself; I had one day to take finals and somehow it was the only day I had other plans. I woke up that morning around 6 A.M. in serious pain. I went to CVS to get some heavy pain medication, came home, and rested while I studied. Later, still in my pajamas and not feeling too well, I dragged Hannah with me to look at the new futon.

It was the shadiest thing I had ever done. I drove into a weird apartment complex way off campus, rang the doorbell and, after much waiting, a long-haired scraggly man appeared to let me in.

Thank GOD I had brought Hannah.

I paid him the money for it, and without his help, Hannah and I dragged the sofa down to my 2 door Ford Explorer. We had to put both of the back seats flat on the ground, scrunch the driver's and the passenger's seats forward, and even though I drove with the steering wheel imbedded into my internal organs, we got the futon home.

But there was no way in hell we were going to move it into my apartment alone.

Still in pain, I rested in my apartment for a bit, and headed to my first final, which was for my Introduction to Christianity exam.

God must have a serious sense of humor because the instant that I got my exam I thought:

"I am going to be sick."

I thought for sure I was going to vomit on my exam, and what was worse was that it was (gentlemen…prepare yourselves) "that time of the month."

Crap.

"Dear Jesus," I prayed, "It's ironic that I am praying to you during an exam about you…but if you could get me through this, I'd be so grateful."

What was worse was that I could rush through the multiple choice section, just marking off a letter here or there to get me out of the exam as quickly as possible, but the essay was something that I could not bullshit my way through.

I wish I could see what I wrote that day. It had to have been hilarious. My professor must have thought so too, because I got a 79 on the final and I was sure I didn't deserve it.

Thanks for the sympathy/insanity points, sir.

I threw up a little in the bathroom outside the lecture hall and headed to my second exam.

That's right: I still had one more exam to go.

Luckily, at my second exam, I made friends with the guy who sat next to me, and he nicely offered to drive me home, since he had parked in the parking lot outside the lecture hall.

SCORE!

I got home, and James and his friend Jake came over to move my new futon in. When they left, I took a nap.

When had I become so boring?

I spent that night in pure agony. I was so nauseous and dizzy I could not move, and I kept thinking that this was the end of my life. If I died in that single apartment, people might not find me for days or weeks. I would truly die all alone and it was going to happen soon.

I never thought small.

I thought, fleetingly, that perhaps I was allergic to the futon.

WebMD did not list "futon allergy" as a possible ailment.

Fail.

I could not get up to go to the bathroom, could not get up to get myself a glass of Sprite, and I just laid on my futon for hours, crying.

A few hours into this magical adventure, I texted my neighbor Anna to see if she had any Sprite she could bring over. I thought that it might settle my stomach and make me feel better. Because she is amazing, she went to two different stores and returned to my apartment with a two liter of Sprite.

Thank you, Anna!

I was scheduled to drive home the next day, but because of my condition my mom told me to take another day off. Even with my whole day to feel better, I didn't. I drove the following Saturday in pure agony to say goodbye to Hannah, and then drove to West Lafayette to meet my mom and dad.

Usually, I would say that calling that day "pure agony" was overdramatic of me. I tend to think the world is ending even with the smallest thing. But when it comes to pain and physical issues, I tend to downplay things until they get bad. Here, they were bad. Imagine driving two hours with the worst hangover you have ever had. Now, multiply the nausea, headache, dizziness, and irritation by about ten and you have how I was feeling that day.

I met them at Denny's on exit 26 and almost cried when I saw them. I had never needed my parents more in my college experience. I had endured creepy guys, horrible boyfriends, and hospital visits in my three previous years, but this was an awful feeling that I just could not shake.

Something was not right.

When we ordered pancakes and sat down, all I could do was sip my Sprite and nibble on my pancakes.

Brittney Little never lost her appetite.

Something was not right, indeed.

My dad took my car and I rode with my mom the rest of the way home. When we arrived, I spent the next 24 hours sleeping, avoiding food, and sipping on water when I could. It was frustrating because I had no idea what was causing such a terrible feeling. I was scared to go to the bathroom or shower alone fearing that I would faint and hurt myself. I felt like at 21 years old, any responsibility that I gained over the years by being able to take care of myself was gone. I was completely dependent on someone to bring me anti-nausea medicine, glasses of water, and to make sure I wasn't throwing either of those things up.

Basically, it sucked.

The worst part about it was there was no hope. When you have a cold or the flu, you go to bed with the hope that in the morning you feel better. Every morning I woke up I felt the same, if not worse. Sooner or later, Mother's Day rolled around and I knew I had to try and fake feeling better for my mom.

My brother and I were in charge of going to Dairy Queen and getting her an ice cream cake, so I ordered it, showered, and set out to the car with my brother.

But first I had to run into the bathroom and vomit.

My brother didn't seem to want me in his brand new truck, so he went to DQ and I stayed home.

Can't say I didn't try.

We had dinner with my aunt and uncle, as is our Mother's Day tradition, and I suffered through it. All through the dinner I fought back the urge to gag...the smells were making my stomach hurt and the conversation and bustle in the room was making me dizzy.

"You can do it," I pep talked myself, "Don't ruin Mother's Day."

At 9 P.M. that night, when our guests had left, I found myself on the floor of the bathroom vomiting and crying hysterically.

Clearly, I was not getting better.

Again, I called Lizzie's mom for advice. Again, she was worried it was my appendix and sent me to the hospital. So, at 10 P.M. on Mother's Day, my mom and I trekked to the emergency room armed with a blanket and two bottles of water.

And what a long night it would be.

Lesson Number 37: How to avoid an unnecessary liver transplant.

A friend at my church youth group, Doctor Bill, was the only doctor that I had ever trusted up until that point. Doctor Bill, or D-Bill, had been a good friend of our family's for years and had always taken the time to answer any questions that I had, medical or not, and had always gone above and beyond for the teens of our church. So when I found out that I was going to the hospital, he was the first number I called. And the second…and the third…and then I began to panic and think that he was out of town.

Crap.

In the ER, the nurse walked me straight into my own room, where I proceeded to vomit in the sink as the back of my gown flew open.

"Don't look!" I managed to yell between heaves, "I am wearing snowman underwear! I am so embarrassed."

Yeah. I was embarrassed about snowmen underwear, but not about vomiting in the sink of the room I was in.

I needed to get my priorities straight.

Eventually, the nurse came in to administer my IV. Instead of throwing a tantrum this time, I was mentally prepared.

But not physically.

"I am having some issues finding your vein," the nice male nurse said, "so please bear with me."

"Okay," I joked, "I trust you...unless you're a Purdue graduate."

He was.

(Insert foot in mouth.)

So he and I began the age-old argument about which school was better, IU or Purdue, and soon, my IV was in. The worst was over.

Or so I thought.

I was given medicine that stopped the nausea and soon I was feeling a little better. I could finally articulate what was wrong with me, and I was able to joke a little with the doctor. He was an old, round Indian man who talked with a thick accent that took a while for my mom and I to understand. I told him the things that were wrong with me, and he insisted that I was "just like his wife."

I highly doubted that.

The doctor said he would call the ultrasound technician and get an ultrasound of me to see what was going on. That seemed easy enough for me until the nice young lady nurse came in with a catheter.

HELL NO.

I am generally so nice to people. I never tell people "no." I am courteous to people who are trying to help me, but when that lady came in with that THING, I had a panic attack beyond all belief.

"No," I began calmly, "No thanks. Not going to happen. No."

"Well this is the only way we can do the ultrasound," the nice nurse said.

"NO!" I yelled as I began to cry hysterically.

It went in anyways.

I never get what I want.

I told her I trusted her more than the dumb Purdue graduate who was putting in my IV.

"You mean my husband?" she replied.

(And there goes my other foot...)

Then, the Purdue graduate asked me to walk to my ultrasound with the catheter in me.

Again, I politely declined.

"Um. Hell no. Is there any way you could like...wheel me there?"

Finally, I got what I wanted.

So, feeling like a princess, I was wheeled across the hallway to the ultrasound room, waving to the nurses and other patients as I went. I got to meet Kate, the ultrasound technician who was fun to talk to, and she took some pictures and things of my organs…or whatever ultrasound people do. Meanwhile, it was around 3:00 A.M. and I was texting Michael. He was staying up really late to talk to me and was really calming me down.

Until the doctor came back with the results and did not look too happy.

"You're liver enzymes are dangerously high," he said referring to my blood test, "But your ultrasound looks normal. We are going to take your catheter out and do an ultrasound of your liver to see what's going on up there and take a look at your gallstones."

Ever hear what your liver sounds like?

I have!

Sadly (and I say "sadly" because I just wanted answers for my health issues) both my liver and gallbladder looked normal, meaning the reason behind my liver enzyme elevation was unknown. Then, the questions really began.

"Have you been on a drinking binge lately?"

"No."

"Have you possibly been exposed to hepatitis?"

"No."

We were not getting anywhere.

I had a hepatitis test (which was negative) and suddenly they were stumped.

And I was pissed.

"I want to go home!" I whined pathetically.

I was handling this all so well.

The doctor explained to me that I could go home, but if my liver enzymes did not go down I would possibly go jaundice and be on the liver transplant list in a few days or weeks. He had said that the level my enzymes were at was dangerous, and that liver damage could not be reversed.

Now who's being dramatic? Geez.

At some point during all of this, I had revealed that I had still been periodically taking the Vicodin I had earlier been prescribed to deal with the pains I was having from my cysts.

Upon hearing that I had been taking Vicodin, my doctor went to the worst possible scenario. Even though I was taking half the recommended dose of the drug, and even though I only took it once a month or so, the doctor believed that I had given myself acetaminophen poisoning, which can potentially damage your liver. He called poison control, and I was told I needed to be monitored.

Even though there was no acetaminophen in my blood or liver when they tested me.

So I hopped into the ambulance and headed to another hospital, only this time in the ambulance I did not get a guy's phone number.

I guess that only happens once in a lifetime.

I even offered to buy the EMT's and the ambulance driver coffee, but told them that my wallet was in my other gown.

They didn't laugh.

Tough crowd.

When I arrived to the hospital, I was placed in the children's ward. Yes, I was a 21 year old in the children's ward. The nurse had to ask me questions she never got to ask her other, younger, patients.

"Do you drink? And how often? Are you sexually active?"

I bet the 6 year old down the hallway did not have to deal with that awkwardness.

On the bright side, I got to have a ton of Jello and Sierra Mist. So I guess the day wasn't a total loss.

On the down side however, I was still left without answers, still stuck with an uncomfortable IV in my arm, and still clad in a hospital gown.

You win some, and you lose some.

I was just about to doze off after being up all night when my phone rang.

It was Doctor Bill!

Basically, what my friend D-Bill told me was that if they weren't treating me (which they were not) and if they had no idea what was wrong with me (which they did not), that I should ask them to release me and come to him for a consultation. If I could get copies of everything that they did to me, he would review them and maybe he could figure out the mystery to my nausea, my increased liver enzymes, and my pain over the past few months.

Eventually, they released me. I got to put on my ratty white pajama pants, old fraying green tee, and my black flip flops and headed out into the sunlight and to the car. I was free, but not safe. We didn't know when the pain was going to come back and I was worried that it would. I got home, showered (thank GOD), and changed into clean sweatpants and my Hoosierette warm-up jacket. It was my most "shabby chic" outfit I had and it just felt good to wear clothes like an adult, as opposed to a gown.

It's always the simple things.

D-Bill is a miracle man. Ten minutes into his house call, he asked me if anyone had done a mono test on me.

No, no they had not.

The next day I found out that I had acute Epstein-Barr virus. Basically, I had raging mono.

Should have seen that coming.

It was then that I began to go to a regular doctor and be seen by Kathy, the nurse practitioner.

After seeing her and getting a lovely shot of steroids in the ass, I was ready to fight this thing. And I did.

For 5 weeks.

Lesson Number 38: How to make no money and have no fun

That's right. For five whole weeks I stayed on the couch watching Netflix movies, coloring in a Princess coloring book, and planning out Hoosierette excursions for the fall. It sounds like a luxury, being able to sleep whenever you want, but in reality it sucked. It was summer, so I couldn't go out and do fun summery things yet, and the constant drowsiness was more or less like narcolepsy. I always fell asleep when I did not want to, I was always too tired to drive anywhere, and I was really lonely.

And so began "The Summer of Healing."

Slowly, I was permitted to get up and do things. I could do errands with my mom one day. I could go with her to lunch another day. Then I was allowed to go places with my friend Kelly. So, occasionally I would go to breakfast with her or go to the youth group's softball games with her and my brother, who was the coach. Then I was allowed to drive and then, after all of that, I was allowed to go on a trip to Kentucky.

The idea wasn't exactly my own. I had gone to Harlan County, Kentucky every year I was in high school to build and rehabilitate houses for the needy. It was the most rewarding thing I had done in my high school years, and I had vowed that I would go again if I ever got the chance as a young adult. With my jobless summer and just coming out of being sick, Christine, our parish's youth minister, suggested I think about going.

I was SO in.

But I had a lot of anxiety about my health.

The trip was the best circumstances I could imagine. D-Bill was going, for starters – meaning any nausea could be managed by him. Christine was obviously going and she always had looked out for me like a second mom. But I was still worried about not being able to give 100 percent and feeling not up to it.

Lesson Number 39: Sometimes a change in scenery gives a change in perspective.

Because I was a young adult, I was permitted to drive the suburban that one group gets to take. I cannot express enough how much I love to drive. I-65 is my playground, I have been off every exit of that highway with all of my years driving to and from Bloomington. After a quick mass to bless our journey, I was in heaven behind the wheel and on our way to do something so great.

Harlan, Kentucky is nestled in the Appalachian Mountains. The drive up there is nothing less than gorgeous, with the elevation and beautiful bodies of water all around. Pulling through the town, it was hard for me to catch my breath. This is where I last felt myself. This place was where I first started writing songs and learning how to play guitar. This was the place where I experienced hard work and service for the first time. This place linked my brother and me, as he had spent many weeks here too as a teen. I loved this town. It had such magic to me, even though I had not been back.

Until now.

As we pulled into the driveway of Camp Sleepy Hollow, we all smiled a little. No matter how much each of us had changed over the years, this place never did. The first cabin is a small wooden cabin with a concrete front porch, the second cabin was two stories and small and thin, and the third cabin (my favorite) was more like a sorority's "cold dorm." We all slept in tons of bunk beds with little personal space – all in the same room, with just two bathrooms in the place. It's silly, but it's such a bonding experience and it really makes the whole week complete.

That was exactly where I planned to sleep.

Unpacking the cars, the trucks, the vans that transport all of the volunteers to Kentucky...it is always a challenge, but we got settled and the college kids set up dinner and got the camp all set up. This would be our home for the next week, and all of us needed to work together to make the experience go smoothly.

Oh yes, this was going to be a week to remember.

Our service project for that week was to rehabilitate the campsite where we stayed. We put in new floors, we painted bunk beds and walls, and we cleaned. Oh goodness, did we all clean. I made friends with the people I did not know in my group and rekindled some old youth group friendships that week.

But beyond all of that was Theo.

Theodore means "Gift from God" and that he was. He was broad-shouldered and tanned from working hard quite often. He had many rugged characteristics: he liked tractors and working with his hands, as well as hunting and, in spite of that, he and I became pretty good friends. He was easy to talk to and understood me, since his sister and I were a lot alike and he and I had been through some similar situations. We didn't have a ton in common, but I was instantly comfortable around him because he reminded me a lot of my brother, Johnny. It was our growing friendship, mine and Theo's, that reminded me that Johnny and I could still be friends. It was Theo and his sister's inspiring friendship that reminded me that my brother and I were all we had in this world. It was a valuable lesson that I was lucky to learn.

We spent our days pushing ourselves to do our best. We plowed through all of our projects and drilled ourselves all day, but at night we lounged at the beach and helped ourselves to extra popsicles that were kept in the freezer.

I wished that I could stay there all summer. I felt healthier there on my weakest days than I did at home. Something about that mountain air, or that Appalachian magic, I guess. It was there that I started writing songs again and that I realized that I had changed since high school.

Everyone changes, sometimes for the better, but sometimes not, and I wondered if maybe my changes were negative. I looked around at these people who were so wholesome like I was in high school, and so invested in doing the right thing, and I worried that I was losing touch with that particular quality.

It was then that I set my sights on graduation and getting out of town. I needed to finish college and go back to being the person I was before my university experience ruined me. I needed to get my priorities straight.

That was becoming a theme.

In the middle of the week, we had mass in a pavilion overlooking a beach, a lake, and some mountains. After going to mass in such a place, you never want to go inside again. That year, our pastor had the opportunity to be there for the first time, and through his discussion of his awe and wonder at our service, it struck me that this was an essential part of me that I would not want to let go.

Plus, I had gotten a kick ass tan.

I will go back to Harlan as much as possible, I owe it everything. It set my life back on course again. I knew I needed to find my happiness again, and upon our return I set out to do just that.

I really do think too big.

And so, after a few life-altering lunches with Theo and my other Kentucky friends, I found my way back to Bloomington, searching for a purpose and direction.

But, where do you start?

Senioritis is Contagious and Incurable: Senior Year

Graduation is not something to look forward to. It's something that looms over you. For some, the dread begins freshman year, with wonders of what one might do after that important milestone. For others, it does not begin until senior year. It's a growing dread...graduation seems so far away when you're 18. But there I was, 21, and the date was set. Where was I going after college? My immediate thought, my fallback option, was going to Nashville, Tennessee to follow my dream of being a country music star. But the rationality of a college senior was setting in. And suddenly, a lifetime of internet surfing in my parent's house seemed to be all that I was qualified for. At the time, I felt entirely alone. Everyone seemed to know where they were going to be after graduation. Everyone, that is, except for me.

But I did begin senior year knowing one thing for sure: it had to be easier than my junior year.

As for my "find happiness" plan, I figured it would start by achieving my dreams.

Senior Year Rule 1: Tie up loose ends and fight for what you want. It's your last chance.

Before the school year had begun, the "executive board" of Hoosierettes and I met to discuss the plan of action we would take going into the following year. Our plan was to "fake it 'til we make it," and be as professional as possible. We were all seemingly on the same page heading into the "recruitment season."

Our biggest event for drawing in new members is IU's "Student Involvement Fair." The Student Activities Organization sets up a ton of tables and chairs in the parking lot of the student union, and different organizations offer information about their groups. The girls and I all had shifts and (even though I missed a little bit of class) we ended up with 77 interested members.

In the previous year, we had 12 girls pay, and only 6 girls remained at the end of the year. So when I had the opportunity for 77 people, I was thrilled. Obviously, they wouldn't all be entirely committed and not all of them would want to try out, but that was a lot of interested people. I scrambled to find a bigger practice space so we could accommodate more girls, but, in the end, we could only take about 25 girls. Tryouts were in order, a date was set, and we were ready.

This was going to be our year.

We had the next few months scheduled, and set high standards and expectations. Finally, we ended up taking 23 special girls for the team.

I was on top of the world. I was talking to Michael again; I was the captain of an amazing dance team. I was living the life.

Except I had kind of forgotten about school.

You see, I was starting to feel like Hoosierettes was my major, and college was my minor. I ate, slept, drank, and basically lived Hoosierettes. I checked my email each morning to see if the girls needed anything, spent extra time making schedules and calling the Athletic Department, and nearly stalked the "executive board" that consisted of my veteran dancers. My life was wrapped up in this team, and I was convinced that we were going to make it. We had to. The school newspaper did an article on the Hoosierettes and our struggle for recognition on campus, and shortly after I had a meeting with not one, not two, but three athletic directors. The article said that we had never heard back from the Athletic Department about any of our performance inquiries, and they were interested in hearing our point of view.

Senior Year Rule Number 2: You might be "over the hill" in the college world.

When we realized that I was getting a little Hoosierette crazy, Hannah and I headed out on the town more often. I needed to get out of my single apartment and out of Hoosieretteland, and we both needed to live up our last few months in Bloomington. One night, we were at Hannah's house having a party and just getting a little buzzed playing beer pong and listening to music. Everyone was really chill, and we were having a lot of fun.

Until our friend Ian sat down and broke a glass table.

He didn't mean to, but the repair would be costly and it was decided (ahem...determined by Hannah) that we would not be partying much that semester at Hannah's house.

A different night, Hannah and I headed back to our old stomping grounds: the off-campus fraternity. Even that was a weird experience. We walked in and barely knew anyone, and somebody's mother was partying there! Seriously! A 40-something year old was there, living it up. What had we walked in to?

Were our partying days behind us? Were we becoming old cat ladies?

Oh the horror!

I was in a rut. I was becoming a cat lady. I was never going to have fun.

Then Michael, one of my only sources of fun, called me to tell me that he was being sent to the East Coast to aid in the hurricane relief. He wouldn't be able to talk for a while, but he had always promised that he would say goodbye when he left.

It was my goodbye phone call, and I was devastated.

I spent a week so worried about him and wondering if he was okay. I missed his random visits, his late night texts...I missed my best friend. I was worried he wasn't coming back.

I had my meeting with the Athletic Department to focus on and, with Michael being gone, I threw myself into it. I researched each of the directors that would be attending the meeting, and what their job entailed, added information to the portfolio I had on the team, and picked out a classy outfit.

With my bangs pulled back and my hair piled up high, I headed into the department's beautiful office facilities. I wore a long sleeved black dress and caramel colored high heeled boots. I was dressed for success.

Except I was pouring sweat.

These three guys were the most official and most important people I had ever had to meet. I felt like they determined my future, but, more importantly, the futures of the 23 girls I had grown to really care about. When we all shook hands and sat down in the conference room (I know, right?), I took a look around and panicked a little. There we were, the four of us in a conference room that seated twenty, having a business meeting.

Was I finally a grown up?

The meeting went decently, as the men asked a lot of questions and clarified a lot of information for us. The team would not be sanctioned that year, but I was applauded for my hard work and they would continue to work with us on possible performance events.

A few weeks later, Michael texted me back, telling me that he never left. It was a false alarm but he had been too busy to text me and tell me.

Sometimes he can REALLY tick me off...

So I adjusted my focus off of him and back onto Hoosierettes and my health. I was feeling physically good, but mentally I was a mess. I hated everyone, I was grouchy all the time, and some days it took everything I had not to cry before I got home. I couldn't figure out what was wrong. I was generally a happy person.

Who was I becoming?

Senior Year Rule Number 3: Figure shit out before you're off of your parents' insurance.

I had always been a worrier, but now it was at an extreme. My mind was noisy with concerns,

"What if I never get a job?"

"What if I am never happy again?"

"What if Michael and I lose touch?"

"What if my parents secretly resent me for how much money my degree is costing them?"

It never stopped.

I wanted to tell Hannah about all of these problems, but she was dealing with issues of her own, being a senior and beginning her own Mary Kay business. Of course I wanted to tell Lizzie too, but I hadn't heard back from her in months. I felt like I was all alone.

Except, of course, for Michael.

Michael knew exactly what I was going through and was being so supportive. He told me that I could talk to my doctor about it and maybe finally get a diagnosis, but he seemed to believe I had an anxiety disorder.

After a phone call to my doctor, she confirmed that Michael was correct. All the noise and the worry in my head accompanied by the periodic sadness were finally explained, and I could get started on learning techniques to manage them.

Senior Year Rule Number 4: Everyone is having issues... you aren't alone.

But I wouldn't tell my friends.

After having all of the health issues I had had that summer, I did not want to be viewed as "weak" to anyone. I kept my secret with Michael alone, studied websites and psychology journals in seclusion, and began to work on my new obstacle.

The key to battling my anxiety, I discovered, was keeping busy and finding things to do when my thoughts were getting the best of me. I threw myself into Hoosierettes, watched movies to unwind before bed, and wrote in my journal or redesigned my bottle-top-coffee-table when my thoughts began to overwhelm my mind.

Because of this realization, my transition into my senior year was my hardest one yet. Trying to deal with the anxieties, my health issues, the budding Hoosierettes, and keeping all of my stress a secret from my friends was difficult. But I survived. I made it through September and October with a lot of struggle, but once the Hoosierettes' biggest performance week was upon us, I was on top of things.

Our season's kick off is always Homecoming Week. It's the most stressful time for me, but it is always one of the most fun times as well. As suggested by the fraternity I had grown so close with, the two groups were having many events together, all of which were hosted by the fraternity. These events all culminated in the team's first two performances, as well as voting for a Hoosierette Homecoming Queen and Court at the end of the week.

As the nerves of the week mounted, the fun of the week did too. Practice was stressful on Monday, with the team distracted by the events that occur on campus during Homecoming Week. Tuesday the girls and I traveled to the fraternity to sit outside on couches with pillows and blankets and watch a scary movie under the stars. With the sky completely clear, and the air crisp and cool, and all of my teammates and friends around me, I had no idea how life could get better.

Talk about low anxiety.

Wednesday I arrived at practice carrying four tiaras and sashes that I had worked so hard finding and creating. Someone had given me the brilliant idea to keep the girls working hard by having the teammates vote for a Hoosierette Queen, Princess, and court. We were all eligible for the awards and all of the girls seemed excited. We had our voting, and as we all sat down to hear the results read by two volunteer teammates, I had another amazing moment.

We were finally a team.

As Taylor and Abby were voted the Homecoming Court, and their teammates hugged them, I realized that aside from the performance opportunities that I had wanted for us, the team itself was amazing. We were all friends, all having fun, and all of us cared for one another. For a moment, I didn't care who won the tiara and the honor of being the hardest worker of the team, I was just glad that we all were a real team.

Earth to Brittney. Earth to Brittney.

In the midst of this warm and fuzzy realization, I won the Hoosierette Homecoming Queen.

I had never been so proud of myself. I had never been so happy to be a part of this team. For the first time, I felt like all of the work I did putting schedules together, answering emails until 4 A.M....all of it was actually appreciated.

Plus, for all of that, I got a sparkly crown.

I was WINNING!

I was walking on sunshine through the party that evening. I had never spent a lot of time with the girls outside of the practice room, and, oh my Lord, were they a funny bunch. Raven was getting down on the dance floor, Rebekah was dancing with wild abandon, and Lizzie was loosening up with a few drinks. I loved that everyone was jamming out and having fun. I loved that I could share these moments with these amazing girls. I loved Homecoming Week.

I can't believe I was sober while I was having these thoughts.

Because of my liver damage that previous summer, I was very wary about drinking. While I would have loved nothing more than to grab a few drinks to loosen up, I realized that my health was more important. I had also realized that alcohol did not really help the anxiety thing.

Being sober had become my lot in life.

By the time Thursday night of Homecoming weekend had rolled around, I needed a break. Michael was having some issues up in Indianapolis, so after driving all of the girls to the fraternity's cook out, I packed a bag, got in my car, and headed to see him.

Being in Indy with Michael always recharged me. It was my mini vacation home. It was the perfect place to get away. Michael generally slept on his couch, so I always got to sleep in his super comfortable full-sized bed with the super soft jersey sheets. It was like staying in a hotel, only I got someone to snuggle with, I got to watch Disney movies and all the TV I wanted, and I got to eat some amazing food.

The only problem with Michael's place was leaving.

Michael worked downtown and needed to be awake at 5:30 A.M. He warned me of this each time I came, but after the first trip I had realized that he only wanted the OPTION of being awake at 5:30 A.M. The alarm would go off, I would hear it from his room and come running, only to find him sound asleep. 5:45 was a similar situation, then 6:00, then 6:15, and finally, around 6:30, he would begin to stir. Meanwhile, I would be fully dressed and made-up, channel surfing, and occasionally sitting on him to get him to wake up.

I was such a lovely house guest.

I'd grab two Mountain Dews from the fridge (one for him, one for me), we'd head to the still-dark apartment complex parking lot, and with a big hug and a honk of the car horn, we would both be off; he to work and I back to Bloomington.

A drive at 6:45 A.M. usually put things in perspective for me, but as I headed back into Homecoming Weekend Chaos (that's right, capitalization again) I began to panic.

"What if we didn't do well in the parade?"

"What if someone does not show up?"

"What if I mess up the times?"

"What if I oversleep for something?"

That damn anxiety was making its way into my peaceful 7:00 A.M. drive.

I returned safely into Bloomington to take a nap, only to wake up to a text message from a fellow Hoosierette a few hours later.

"Hiiii," Annette's text said.

A bubble of panic rose up in my chest. Was I running late? Was she looking for me to start the Homecoming Parade? I hadn't showered yet! I hadn't put on lipstick yet!

Then I realized it was only around noon and I wasn't due at the parade for another five hours.

"Um hi?" I responded.

I had forgotten we had a date to get our bangs trimmed.

Anxiety averted.

5:00 P.M. had to roll around eventually though. After decorating our parade vehicle, being out of gas and late to the parade, piling seven girls into my small SUV, and searching for my elusive lipstick, we had made it to the parade site. The team performed amazingly and, with fans cheering on either side of the street, we were all beaming.

One performance of the weekend down and one to go.

The next morning we were scheduled to perform at 10:00 A.M. at the Bloomington Farmer's Market. Rides for each Hoosierette were all planned, and I was in charge of picking up the dancers that were in one of the sorority houses. I texted them all when I arrived at 9:15 and waited. One by one, they ran down the steps – a few of them had been awakened only by my text! We were all discombobulated that morning. In spite of the exhaustion, in spite of the redundancy of the weekend, we still had a fun time just jamming out in the farmers market in the 40 degree weather.

I could not love this team any more.

After surviving Homecoming Week with my anxiety, I thought I was the queen of college. I had a great team, I had great friends, I was finally back on track from my rocky transition back to school. The only problem I was still having was graduation.

Laugh if you must, but up until my senior year I honestly thought I could be a songwriter. Michael and I had discussed the realities of the situation, and I had researched the probability of it, but I thought I could do it.

I didn't yet have a back-up plan: a realistic choice for the rest of my life.

Senior Year Rule 5: Dealing with facing the (lack of) workforce.

I never wanted to research my plan B. Who does? Everyone wants their dreams to come true, and only a few people are fortunate enough to go off and chase them.

I was not yet brave enough to take a chance on songwriting.

So I searched for an alternative. Would I work as an athletic director or a dance coach? Would I work in a boring cubicle doing filing or whatever people do in cubicles?

Time to figure out my future.

One time, back in freshman year an advisor asked me what I wanted to do for the rest of my life to determine what classes I could take during my collegiate career.

"Well, I was just planning on getting implants and becoming a trophy wife," I had joked back then.

Now, as a senior, that seemed like a good idea.

I'm not the kind of person who can just do whatever I am told to do, just to make money. I want to be doing something I love, something I know can make a difference, and I want to be happy.

Being rich wouldn't be a bad bonus, either.

What could an English major with a psychology minor do with the rest of her life? What was she qualified for?

BESIDES drinking heavily and quoting *Othello?* Nothing, it seemed.

I have always known I was going to be famous. Seriously. It was not just a dream for me, I could see it. I could see myself going on "Regis and Kelly" talking about my most recent book or upcoming music tour. I could see myself taking a tour to France and to Spain with a car and a busy itinerary of things to do and people to see. I could even see myself paying off my parent's bills and my student loans with the money I was making.

The problem was this: what was I going to become famous for?

Was I a good enough singer, actress, writer, or dancer to do any of these things professionally?

Well, I sure didn't think so.

Mental strength was clearly not one of my dominant features.

Anyways, college was going better, at least as far as the Hoosierettes and my anxiety were concerned, and I was really buckling down on my homework and studies. I even had most of my professors pretty figured out...

Or so I thought.

Senior Year Rule Number 6: Hating everyone is okay…the old and senile can do that.

Professor Roberts had it in for me. Of that I was certain. He had a beard and a cloud of curly hair and looked like how you would imagine an English professor to look. He wore blazers with suede elbow patches and used obscenely big words whenever possible.

Oh yeah, and he hated me.

First he started calling me Tiffany every once in a while. I thought it was a mistake, but it didn't make any sense. There were two Brittneys in the class and no Tiffanys. If you were to take a shot in the dark and call a girl a name in the class, you should have picked Brittney.

He continued to call me Tiffany.

Then, there was the issue of emails. These days in college, teachers and students rely on emails as an essential form of communication. Teachers expect students to respond to emails in a timely manner, and students expect the teachers to do the same.

Not Professor Roberts.

He never once emailed me back the entire semester to my inquiries about missed classes and the syllabus.

Rough life.

Other than Professor "Thinks-he's-funny-and-calls-me-Tiffany-but-doesn't-email-Brittney-back" (or Roberts for short), I had seriously thought that with persistent attendance and investment in my education that semester I would end up dramatically increasing my GPA.

A few assignments in, I realized that Professor Roberts would not grant me that GPA.

Welcome back, anxiety, my old friend. This episode of insane fear, obsessively studying, and resulting anger is brought to you by Mick Roberts of the English department.

Bastard.

With the end of November fast approaching, the Hoosierettes needed to gear up for another performance, this one made of my own brilliance. The girls were to come to the IU vs. Purdue game for maximum exposure and perform as much as possible around the stadium area!

Senior Year Rule Number 7: Pull a "Jesus." Instead of preaching whenever and wherever... you can just stick to what you know.

Sometimes, my genius is just too good.

The game was traditionally after Thanksgiving, so on my way back from break I stopped in to see Michael. He was at a bar in Indianapolis with a few of his older friends and asked me to stop in and visit.

Chris and Frank, Michael's older friends, weren't the accommodating type. I spent two hours feeling awkward and wanting to leave, but not wanting to offend Michael. I tried to be nice and talk football, or TV, or anything with them. They didn't seem to appreciate the effort. At the end of the visit I was exhausted from trying. I got up to leave with Michael when Chris said to him,

"Oh you've got to leave with your bitch?"

Um. Excuse me? Bitch?

"No offense," Chris added hastily, but not laughing or taking his eyes off me for a minute.

I had never been called a bitch to my face in my life, especially from someone I had barely spent time with. Sure, when I was defensive about something or felt like I had been wronged in some ways I could have some bitchy tendencies…but I had never been told this before. Ever.

Needless to say, the small comment from the insignificant source got under my skin.

"Do you think I'm a bitch?" I pondered as Michael and I strolled through the cool, organized aisles of the grocery store later that evening.

"Did that seriously bother you?" he asked me. "He jokes like that all the time…Chris didn't mean anything by it."

That only subdued me for a few hours.

"Are you sure that like…everyone doesn't think I am a bitch but they just don't tell me like Chris did?" I later texted Michael that evening.

I needed to learn how to let things go.

And I did for a while, because the next morning I needed to get up at 7:00 A.M. and be "game day" dressed for the tailgate. The Hoosierettes had a lot of preparations to tend to and, of course, I had barely even started things.

Rebekah, Annette, Michelle, and Hannah seriously went above and beyond that morning. The girls and I bought sandwiches, sodas, set up the tailgate site, and got everything ready in record time. I couldn't have done it without them. Around noon, all decked out with our crimson warm-ups and cream colored hair bows, and our faces made up complete with dark lipstick and thick eyelashes, the girls and I headed into the amazing IU vs. Purdue tailgate.

Again, one of those moments hit me. Sitting around the tailgate, eating sandwiches and laughing with my teammates, I thought that it was perfect. My amazing teammates and I were all there and ready to prove ourselves to the campus as a serious team. We had family members visiting us and watching us perform, and we were making friends with the tailgates around us. This team, a team that had started as a dream of mine, was becoming a success.

That day was a success too. We walked around in our beautiful warm-ups with our heads held high. We took photos with tons of little girls who looked star-struck as we performed. We danced with the Athletic Department watching, and we made the Purdue band stop and stare. We even had some time on national television, waving our poms even when our team was losing. IU ended up losing to Purdue, but the Hoosierettes had won the day. We received the recognition that we so desperately wanted, and we had proved to ourselves that we were serious.

Now, on to the academic success I craved before I graduated. After my epic GPA failure my freshman year in college, I had a lot of digging to do to get my GPA out of that hole. In my senior year, I realized I only had a few more chances to do so. I wanted to bring my GPA up to a 3.0 with just my grades that fall semester, and I calculated that if I got mostly A's with one B I would be able to do so.

Immediately, I planned on that B being in Professor Roberts' class. He had given me mainly C pluses on my papers, writing tons of illegible comments in the margins. When I got a B plus on a paper, he still had comments on the side, saying that the paper wasn't that good.

WHAT DID THIS MAN WANT FROM ME?

So I set out to work harder in class: showing up more, reading harder, looking over my papers to see what I did wrong (which was stupid of me, because that professor's writing was impossible to read), and studying for weeks for the final. I re-read every text on the exam, scoured the notes I had taken, and worked with a friend in my class in the hours before the exam on what to remember.

I got a C minus in the course.

Academic dreams were shattered.

Thanks Professor Roberts.

When I asked him how I got a C minus, he patronizingly emailed me back the formula for calculating my grade.

Thanks, jerk.

I have had plenty of experience failing when I didn't do enough, but when I don't do well after trying my best, I get crushed. I came home from that semester with no relief, no sense of accomplishment in my many other sufficient grades, but rather dwelling on the terror of the one grade I had wanted so badly and just couldn't attain.

Rough life.

But, home was where I needed to be, and I came home ready to rest.

It's weird coming home after living alone. Usually, when I wake up, I alone can decide the fate of my day. If I want to rest all day, I can lie down and watch television all day. If I want to run errands, I can do that, but only when I want to. I am not at the mercy of anyone else.

At home, one must learn to be courteous to those around one.

Because my parents have sacrificed so much to help me go to school and be successful, I owe them a lot. I am so grateful for them, and will honestly do anything they ask of me to help out.

But sometimes, it's hard for me to get my butt off the couch.

Isn't every college student like that?

But I did my mom's bidding whenever she asked me to. I drove to the bank, I got her car washed, and I picked up things at the grocery store whenever she wanted. I couldn't say no.

Not that my mom and I didn't have a good relationship. We watch movies together and always have fun when we run errands. I can generally tell her everything (or at least 99 percent of things), and I liked being home with her.

It's just so DIFFERENT being home.

My brother and I share a bathroom in my house. That is literally the only downside to living in Chicago. If anyone has had to share a bathroom with a boy that is not your betrothed, then you know what I mean. Brothers do not care about impressing you or keeping you happy. A few wet towels lying around could send me off the edge, as he well knew. John always pushed my buttons when I was home, and he always got a rise out of me. It was our thing, no matter how frustrating it was, and after the first little argument I always knew I was home.

Senior Year Rule Number 8: The power of your thoughts is amazing.

Lizzie announced that December that she was going to host a dinner party and naturally, my mom volunteered me to bring a dessert. So my mom decided to make a red velvet cake for me to bring. She (as all good mothers do) let me lick the beaters free of cake batter and let me have the scraps that she didn't use. I was in red velvet heaven. My mouth and fingers were covered in red dye and I couldn't have cared less. It was sheer bliss. Later that evening, my parents went to bed and when I went to the bathroom later that night, something was wrong. Everything that came out of my body was blood red and I had no idea why.

The last time something like this had happened, I ended up in the hospital. The hospital is like jail; once you're there you never want to go back.

"I don't want to go back," I moaned, mostly to myself.

I talked myself down and decided that if it happened again I would tell someone. So when it happened again, I texted my brother. He came downstairs to talk to me and started asking me questions about how I was feeling.

Suddenly I got dizzy, and then nauseous, and before I knew it I was on the floor of the bathroom heaving into a toilet.

How come all of my stories contain some version of that sentence?

My dad got me off the floor and onto the couch, calmed me down and my mom told me what had happened.

"It was from the red velvet cake…the food dye," she explained, "I had the same thing happen to me."

I wasn't bleeding internally at all; I was just getting rid of all the red stuff in my stomach.

How embarrassing!

I had worked myself into such a panic attack because I thought that I was dying that I had gotten myself dizzy and nauseous. I had the power to do that with just my mind.

Freaky.

After talking to a doctor about what had happened, I found out that large amounts of red dye number 40 is actually bad for you and that was what was in the cake!

Needless to say, I have not eaten red velvet cake ever again.

My medical dramas aside, my winter break went much smoother than my summer break had. I wasn't doing much (not having kept in touch with a lot of my high school friends), but I did begin planning out what I was going to do with the rest of my life.

Senior Year Rule Number 9: Follow your dreams and seek inspiration wherever possible.

I had always dreamed of being a country superstar, and had always kept it as an option in the back of my mind. I could literally see myself on tour, running to the studio to work on tracks, and even rehearsing with the group that I was the opening act for. I could feel the spotlight on my face and the bass thumping as I stepped out on performance night, winning the crowd over with my personality and my music. If I could feel and see all these things, it had to come true.

Right?

On the other hand, I had been very well educated at IU and had seen all of the different things that my education could bring. I saw students who went on to graduate school, students who had gotten internships wearing patent leather heels and button down cardigans. That reality I could deal with, but it was not what I loved. I would be safe and secure, but I would always wonder what could have happened if I "caught a break."

Maybe I was complicating it too much, maybe I should have just stuck with what I knew was the easier path, but since when do I like to keep things boring?

UGH!

On Christmas Day, I took a break from my life's planning and went, as we always did, to the movies with my family and our neighbors. The adults went to see "War Horse" leaving the kids to go to "Young Adult."

Watching Charlize Theron on the big screen sleeping until 10, drinking Diet Coke, doing "Just Dance," and then (and only then) heading over to her computer to write was an inspiration. The character she was (falsely) depicting was an author.

That was it.

I had been reading since I was four years old. I have always loved words. I have been telling stories since I was a kid in such an entertaining manner and I have kept hundreds of journals. I mean, I was an English major for Christ's sake…it made sense.

I was going to be an author.

I always began these endeavors like they are so simple.

Add to the list of dreams becoming published and recording an album.

2012 was going to be a busy year…if I could keep my anxiety in check.

The thing about having an anxiety disorder is that you can't control it, and your efforts at minimizing the problem don't always work. For example, over that winter break I set out to clean my closet. The job only took an hour, as I am generally a clean person, but somewhere in the middle of it I started panicking. What if this project couldn't be finished? What If I should be out doing something else? What if everyone hates me for staying in tonight and cleaning my closet?

It seems like a series of irrational fears, and, looking back on it, that can be true. But at the time, the chain of consequences of one action or one possible action seems so great, that just cleaning your closet could change your life.

It's frustrating.

Writing, as I found out, had begun to help with that issue. It seemed that the second that I wrote my issues or anxieties, or even my past or my future worries, that once they hit the paper (or the laptop), they were free from my noisy and anxious mind.

So I began to write. I spent hours writing about my future worries and issues with my past. But interpersonal relationships were what really covered the papers and journals over my desk, and my worries about my friendships began to consume my life.

My mounting anxiety at the time was over my friendship with Michael, which was never stable. Some days he was happy and wanted to chat, some days he wasn't in that kind of mood, or he was simply busy. I tend to take these moods personally. Our personality types are rarely on the same page, and when they are, the time is fleeting. I am the type of person who holds on despite the odds, so when he begins to back off, I press further.

I have a hard time taking a hint.

It was during a period of Michael's withdrawal that I found myself at New Year's Eve of 2012. 2011 had been a year filled with anxiety, mono, and heartbreak. I needed an attitude readjustment for 2012 if I was going to graduate and begin to chase my dreams of writing and singing. New Year's Eve festivities were going to be in Bloomington, so pushing all worry aside I set off on the four hour drive. I didn't know if I really wanted to go. I loved the people on the other end of the trip, but I was worried about kicking off the New Year right. I had tried to secure plans with Michael, was worried about a fall-through in plans with Hannah and James, but somehow, as it usually does, I-65 soothed me, and I found myself in Bloomington.

After an amazing IU basketball win that New Year's Eve, a drink (or several) at Kilroy's Bar, and a party filled with good friends, we said "Hello" to 2012. Later that night, after kicking off my 4 inch heels, stripping out of my tight New Year's ensemble and stepping into sweats, letting my tight bun fall into waves down my back, and scrubbing off my makeup, I had a moment to think about my missteps of 2011, and the triumphs I wanted to have in 2012. I wrote what seemed to be my hundredth song, never to be sung and never to be recorded, and I got mad. The song was great, don't get me wrong, but I was frustrated that my dreams did not seem to be any closer. I needed to make a change. I was no longer going to wait around for things to happen for me, no longer going to grovel for a friendship with Michael, and I was going to live up my last semester of college.

Bring it on, 2012.

At this point, I should probably mention that I had never explicitly told my mom that I was planning on becoming a singer at any cost. I had joked about it and she had too, but I think she was holding out for me to get a "career" – and not in music. I think my poor mother envisioned me wearing slacks and pumps with an ear-bud in as I clomped around an office yelling at someone. Or maybe she saw me wearing khakis and a polo whilst coaching my own pom and dance team. Either way, I don't think at this point she saw me heading to Nashville to sing. So that winter, I let her buy me a suit for job interviews, heels for job interviews, and a purse for job interviews.

But where were these interviews I was dressing for going to be, exactly?

It would be an understatement if I said that I was freaked out at this point in life. I had only really been able to see myself as an entertainer. What if I could not achieve that? What if I was destined to sit in a cubicle or an office for the rest of my life?

See how my anxiety takes over sometimes?

See how I let it?

Sometimes in an anxious situation, it helps to take a minute and think rationally. I prepared a list of things to accomplish before I headed back to school. I started planning out times to visit Indiana University's "Career Development Center," and began sending out job applications for part-time positions that semester and beyond. Having a plan in a "crisis" (or at least it was, according to me) situation is helpful and soothing.

I was armed with a plan. I was armed with 3.5 years of collegiate experience. Dare I say it, but I was actually excited for my final semester of college to begin.

I could only pray that my excitement would last until May.

The Final Semester

It took two weeks for the excitement to die.

The first week of classes, I was walking on sunshine. I was being social, I was looking for jobs, and I was being assured by my friends that it was not at all impossible for me to achieve my dreams of becoming a singer. I visited the career center with vigor, waltzed to each of my classes with cheer, and was beginning to believe that this was actually going to be the best semester of my life.

The second week of classes, Hoosierettes started back up. During the winter break, we had lost two Hoosierettes and I was very sad. One girl was not returning to IU that spring, and one could not handle the team on top of her studies. I could not do anything to stop them from leaving, but I couldn't help but think of the ways in which I might have failed them and the team.

I really need to stop taking things so personally.

Senior Year Rule Number 10: You're the senior, society also dictates that you're the adult.

Twenty minutes before we began the first meeting of the Hoosierettes that semester, I got another email from a girl, quitting. I wasn't surprised. After dealing with a similar situation the prior year, it was apparent with practices and events who would quit mid-year. The girl who emailed me that day had quickly become one of the girls who I could see leaving us very quickly, and she had proved me right.

Just because I wasn't surprised, didn't mean I wasn't mad. I had made it a very big deal at the beginning of the year that a commitment to this team was not something to be taken lightly. Now, I had lost three girls and I was very upset.

Very upset, indeed.

The day after our first team meeting, the Hoosierettes were headed to a women's basketball game to cheer Indiana to victory over Purdue. Earlier that evening, I had gotten yet another email from a Hoosierette, resigning from her position on our team. Four girls in two weeks were too much for me to handle.

This is where my emotions ran away from me.

This is where I get myself in trouble.

As every college girl did in the year 2012, I tweeted my feelings saying, "If you see me on campus, just push me over. Especially if you're a Hoosierette," and, "I hate that nobody can keep their word or believe in commitment."

My feelings were out in the social network; I had named no names, just revealed my frustrations that these things were happening to my team. I had said my piece, and began to get over it.

What I did not anticipate was the reaction of my teammates.

After finding out that more women had quit the team, my teammates were enraged. Here we all were, working hard at making a name for ourselves on campus, planning out dances for 23 girls, and we were down to 19.

They were pissed.

The tweets began innocently enough...girls speaking of their anger against people who back out of a commitment, but it got personal really quickly. They never named names, but the girls began to say things like "I saw her on campus. I am glad she quit, she's ugly." As well as things like, "I didn't like her much anyways."

The most terrible part about this whole thing was not what the girls said in such an easily viewed area of the web...it was that I saw all of this happen, and did nothing to stop it. Nothing at all.

And the worst team captain of the year award goes to...ME.

It didn't occur to me during the game that these girls, the ones who quit, would be upset about the things said online. It didn't occur to me during our teammate's birthday party afterwards that they would say something to me about it. It didn't even occur to me when one of the girls came into the party that this was going to be a conflict or altercation.

Not only am I the worst captain ever, but I was a dumb one too.

The girl who approached me was deceivingly nice. She smiled and waved to everyone, she told me to take my time, and she walked me across the room without any indication as to what was going to happen.

"We saw what had been put online about us, and we showed it to our parents," she began. *Her parents?* I thought to myself, *what could have possibly been said that would require parental supervision?* "My mom has spoken to a lawyer and believes that we have a case for cyberbullying."

WHAT?!

Yeah.

"Um...okay," I stuttered, unintelligently.

"She and I are upset, and we want some sort of repercussions. According to the Respect Policy that YOU wrote, you said that teammates must respect each other and..." she spewed out.

It seemed like she went on forever while I tried to find words.

"I am very sorry that I did not stop the girls when I could have. I am also sorry if I was immature in beginning all of this, and if I had added to it in any way, shape, or form. But you do need to understand, that your teammates are mad that you bailed on them. I know that is not an excuse, but it is where this all begins. You want an apology from the girls who did this, and you deserve that. But I cannot stop them from being angry that they have to work twice as hard for the next few weeks to fix the gaps that you all left behind," I calmly.

That was as professional as I could possibly be.

"Well you have to understand that I was very disappointed in the team. I thought this was a bigger deal, I thought there would be more performances, and I thought that this was going to be more serious," was her response.

Now, according to her, not only was I a cyberbully, but I was a disappointment.

She left after a continually redundant conversation, but I did not shake off her words to me. "Lawyers" and "cyberbullying" and "cases" were not things I cared to think about on my Thursday night out with my team. What was worse was that when I turned around, I had 15 pairs of eyes staring at me as I numbly walked back to the table.

"Does anyone need a ride home?" I asked.

"Umm..." words were mumbled and uncomfortable looks covered faces.

"Yeah," Katherine, one of my executive board members for the team, answered, "I do."

As we walked out of the building, Katherine looked at me and asked me what was wrong. "You look like you are about to cry," she said.

"That's probably because I am," I responded.

As I debriefed her on the incident that had just occurred, my heart sank even further. These girls were my responsibility and I was at fault. I could have stopped this from happening, and I didn't.

Needless to say, I was feeling like a terrible person.

What do all truly terrible people do when they hit rock bottom?

They go to a bar. Or at least I did.

Hannah and I walked into the most crowded evening at Kilroy's Bar I had ever experienced, and vowed that we would only have one drink per person.

Meanwhile, I had texted the girls involved in the "Twitter Scandal of 2012" (yes, this too gets to be capitalized. I thought we had left the capitalization in the past...but obviously not) and told them that we needed to have a meeting the very next day. As they had begun to text me back, my phone had died, so I left it at home.

That didn't mean they couldn't talk to Hannah.

Somehow (and the details are a little blurred by my Long Island Iced Tea), the girls had gotten ahold of Hannah and convinced her and me to drop by on our way back from the bar to explain what had happened and why I was so upset.

I am not sure how it happened on one drink, but by the time Hannah and I got to the impromptu meeting with the "Twitter Terrors," we were buzzed.

Very buzzed.

It was not the most professional way to deal with my issues that day, but the slight dulling of all my senses, in addition to the relief of the anxiety I was feeling about that situation really helped me talk to the girls about what they had done wrong. While they were enraged that their former teammate had hired a lawyer to deal with the situation, they agreed that they respected ME enough to apologize to her.

They weren't going to like it, but they were going to do it for me.

It was in my semi-drunken state that clarity hit me. I was not actually going to go to jail…I had never said anything about her specifically, nor had I ever threatened her. The girls involved, while mean, never mentioned her as well. Besides, as Hannah pointed out in HER buzzed state, who gets a lawyer and has a lawsuit set up in a matter of 4 or 5 hours?

Well, that made me feel a little better.

The next morning though, I had to jump back into "captain mode." I knew that the situation needed to be addressed immediately, and that I was going to have to take responsibility for everyone's actions, including my own. I sent out an email to the current team members as well as the ones who had quit in the past few days:

"Hello Ladies!

As you all know, we have lost a few Hoosierettes in the past few weeks. As the "founder" of this organization, this always causes me great sadness. I love everything about this team, I love all of you, and it's frustrating and depressing to me when girls leave. I realize the reasons for them leaving are diverse, but I always seem to take it personally and I miss each of them and the unique things they all brought to the table.

Yesterday, after receiving an email from a Hoosierette who felt that the team was just too much for her, I felt particularly sad. This happened to us last year (our numbers diminishing after the first semester was over) and it hurt me and the team just as much back then. I had tried so hard to emphasize the importance of commitment in the beginning of THIS year so that this would not happen to us, and yet it was happening again. I worried that I was doing something wrong to cause these changes and to make these girls leave. In anger with myself and with the dropping in numbers I posted a status on twitter about how sad I was that people kept dropping.

What I hadn't anticipated was the anger of the rest of the team that followed my initial tweet. Girls who have worked so hard to keep this team together were suddenly outraged that a lot of their work had failed, upset that they would have to work even harder this semester to fix the team, and depressed that we were having these issues. While I believe that social networks are important to the American freedom of speech, I believe we might have taken things too far in such a public forum.

As punishment for our hasty actions, these girls and I are volunteering more of our time to fund raisers, suspending ourselves from certain Hoosierette privileges, formally apologizing for the hurt that we caused, and moving forward.

I personally, would like to apologize to each and every one of you. The public image of this team has been my number one priority since the day this team began. I regret that I jeopardized that for even a moment, and I hope that you can all accept my sincerest apology.

Another issue that has been brought up in this situation was disappointment. It was mentioned to me that this team was disappointing and that I was not living up to the high expectations that were had for this team. Again, I'd like to apologize. I thought that I had made it clear at the beginning of the year the amount of performances that we would have, as well as the "building" aspect of the team. I honestly had thought that it was clear that we were NOT a sanctioned athletic team, I thought it was clear that we were working toward that goal, and I thought that it was clear (with me giving everyone a tentative schedule) how many performances we would actually have this year. If that was not clear to everyone, and this year has continued to let you down... I am so terribly sorry. All I wanted for this team was for girls to have fun, have the opportunity to perform but most of all MAKE FRIENDS.

In spite of everything that has happened in the past few days, I urge you all to respect the situation at hand. If at all possible, please forgive me for my immature actions and my misleading demeanor through this year, and hopefully we can continue on the amazing journey that I expect us to have this year. I also ask, that we respect the privacy of the girls who we have harmed and keep this episode in the past. We are all ready to move on and we need our team to help us forget about all of this and move towards a better future.

Thank you ladies for your respect and continued dedication through the past few weeks. Please feel free to email me if you have any questions or suggestions on how I can do better and help this team more. I hope I do not disappoint any of you in this way again.

Brittney Little

Hoosierettes Dance Team Captain"

It was the right thing to do. I had learned a valuable lesson that day, and had really grown as a person in that situation.

This episode really made me reflect on my past four years and how much I had matured. Sure, I had threatened a lawsuit on someone freshman year, but my situation was not with a bunch of girls who were mad at me…it was with a guy who would not leave me alone. Had I been on Twitter seeing girls say mean things about me as a freshman, would I have hired a lawyer to scare them? It's hard to say. But I do know that as a senior, I would have done no such thing. As a senior, those kinds of things are petty compared to the threat of graduation and doom of getting a job. I do know that as a freshman, I would not have been able to take responsibility for the harm I had caused and for the disappointment I had been to the girls on the team. I do know that as a freshman, I would not have been able to tell all of the girls what I had done and punish myself for the things I had done wrong.

At least I had a little proof that I was growing up.

Just a little.

That night there was an ice storm. I went out to run a few errands and between a friend's house and my car I had slipped and fell on my already aching wrist.

God was clearly not done punishing me for being such a bad person.

For the rest of the weekend, the fates punished me for what I had done. I had overslept for things, fell on more ice, hit my head on the car door, and much more.

I should have just stayed in bed, never to be seen again.

My friends however, would not let that happen.

And thank God for that.

As a true tribute to friendship, my dance teammates and I had grown closer. Annette, Michelle, Amy and Taylor were as ~~insufferable~~ inseparable as teammates could be. They were a part of the group that created the "Twitter Scandal of 2012," and after we all apologized for our actions to the team and to the girl we had harmed, we were able to bond.

Something like this had never happened on the team before, and I was flying blind with the idea of punishment. The offense, after the initial reaction, was not really that great. Sure, the girls were rude and harsh, but they apologized and the situation was over. We could all put it in the past.

Or so we thought.

At Hoosierettes practice the next week, we prepared for an upcoming performance. The Hoosierettes were finally becoming a big deal and being requested at events. The performance was at the "Miss IU Pageant." Yes, finally, the Hoosierettes were to perform at a legitimate IU event. At practice when I asked the ladies who was able to come to that performance, only a handful of girls raised their hands. In addition to the four who quit and the five who were suspended, this left us with eight girls able to perform and five who were able to be there, but who were suspended from performing due to the "Twitter Scandal."

Suddenly, some of the girls who were able to perform were nervous and shaky, "Do we have to perform with only eight of us?" one asked.

They really didn't.

The reason for the harsh punishment of the five "Twitter Terrors" (including myself) was to ensure the positive image of the team. But if the girls didn't perform, and eight out of nineteen girls were all we could spare for an important IU event, wouldn't we be damaging the team even more?

So the team sentenced us to a ten minute session in the hallway during practice, while they decided our fate. One of our teammates, Kara, pointed out that she as well as many other of our teammates didn't really know exactly what happened and that it was unfair that a bunch of people who didn't know what had happened determine our fate.

Good point there, Kara.

Korin, another dancer, argued that we hadn't been punished enough and that we should not perform. If we did perform, we should have a worse punishment. According to her, we should have been punished even more.

Damn you, Korin.

Eventually Annette, Michelle, Taylor, Amy, and I or the "Cyber Bullies" were allowed to perform in the event.

But a few girls were still unhappy about it.

The girl in charge of our punishment, my friend Katherine, fielded strongly worded emails about the situation, but there was no turning back for her. If we kept going back on our decisions, the team would lose respect for us even more than they already had.

Ugh.

It was dramatic, to say the least. But for the reputation and secure image of the team, we would hold our heads high and stick to our decision.

To reward ourselves for dealing with the drama that had occurred at practice, the "Twitter Terrors" would begin the weekend with a raging party in honor of Annette's birthday. As a co-hostess, I was in charge of buying the liquor, while the rest of them prepared Michelle and Amy's apartment for the festivities.

I drove around to four different stores to find a good bottle of tequila for Annette's birthday present. I drove from one side of town to the other so that the girls could start drinking before I had dinner and got ready. By the time Hannah and I made it to the party, the girls were having a great time.

Senior Year Rule Number 11: How NOT to throw a party.

They had replaced all of the overhead lights with blacklights, decked out the place with glow sticks and neon, and the music was thumping from Annette's badass speaker system. The place was filled with people I did not know, as well as my teammates. Annette was floating around in her birthday best, a cutoff tee shirt, shorts, and high white socks. In the blacklight she was glowing, and from a mile away you could tell that Annette – as well as Taylor and Michelle – were drunk.

Oh, it was going to be a good night.

After a few minutes, Hannah looked bored and told me she was heading out. Somewhere in the depths of my mind I thought that I should leave too and go with her.

I didn't.

Taylor became my wingman after that. I pointed out a guy in a red baseball hat and a yellow shirt to her. He looked like a football player with the biggest arms I had ever seen, dark brown eyes, and a giant bottle of vodka in hand.

"He's hot!" I told Taylor.

"HEY YOU!" she screamed at him, "Come over here!"

Crap.

Immediately I tried to escape.

"Taylor, no. Seriously. No..." I began.

She responded by pinning me behind her and shoving me into the counter.

Thanks, Taylor.

As it turns out, I was right, he was a football player and his name was Donnie.

When would I stop going after guys with dark eyes, large arms, and a love of football?

I am a chicken. No, I am a wuss. I am something, because I cannot talk to boys at parties. I can stand in front of a room full of sorority girls and teach Zumba. I can perform a nationally known ballet in front of thousands. I can write and sing music on the radio with an audience of my peers.

But I cannot talk to boys.

So Taylor bringing over that guy was like pure hell for me. I just couldn't figure out how to start a conversation, couldn't figure out if he was bored with me; basically, I was a mess. So when he later walked away I was relieved.

Then she introduced me to ANOTHER guy, Garrett. When was she going to give up? Luckily she helped me out a little bit more with the second guy and a few drinks in; I was able to articulate a few sentences with the opposite sex.

Thank you, Big Red Liquor Store.

So somehow, I stumbled my way into Michelle's room where a little sub-party was being held. Taylor, Michelle, a few other girls, Garrett, and my new giant football friend Donnie, were in there chatting and hanging out. When Taylor caught sight of me, she whispered into Donnie's ear something and they both pointed at me.

"Get over here!"

I am not really certain how it happened, but he and I began to kiss.

It was wonderful.

Until he turned around and made out with someone else.

Not so wonderful.

I did not realize how drunk he was, until he stumbled over to the bathroom and looked expectantly at all of the girls in the room.

"You okay?" Taylor asked him sarcastically. "Do you need some company in there or something?"

"What?" he asked.

"You know none of these girls are gonna go in there with you. You kissed my friend Brittney, then you turned around and kissed someone else…" she began.

He proceeded to slam the door in frustration.

How attractive…

When he came out, he felt the need to explain things to me.

"I am not like this usually…I am so sorry," he told me, "I am usually a really nice guy. I just wanted to get to know a nice girl. Are you holding my vodka? Can you hold my vodka? Anyways, I like you, you're cute."

"Um…okay. It's gonna be okay. I understand," I told him. "Good luck!" I called at him as he walked away.

I didn't think much of him at all. I didn't think about how drunk he was, or wonder if he was a danger. I didn't think about it – that was, until he began to raise his voice talking to another girl. He didn't seem mad at her exactly, he seemed overexcited about something.

Then he punched a hole in Michelle's bedroom wall.

My standards in men had clearly dropped in college.

It just happened. I don't think he meant it to. He was so large and muscular his arm literally cut through the wall like butter. Suddenly, powder from the drywall covered his hands and the floor and all that was left was a gaping hole. The entire room seemed to go silent for a moment as we all stared in awe.

I looked over at Michelle, and she began crying hysterically. I looked into the hallway as Donnie walked away, as Michelle's boyfriend rushed over to see what happened. What all went on next was a huge blur of violence and confusion. "Boxing Donnie" was leaving the party and, in his drunken state, was denying that he had punched the hole in the wall. Michelle's boyfriend wanted to KILL him, and began screaming and threatening the people who brought Donnie to the party.

Michelle continued to cry and tried to get her boyfriend to calm down.

After "the hole puncher" left the party, we thought things would calm down. A hole in the wall can be patched…it was going to be okay.

*Side Note: I never got this "Donnie" character's last name. For all I know, he is my next door neighbor or something. For all HE knows, he could be reading this right now thinking that he couldn't possibly be the star of this story. Isn't life funny that way?

We thought the party could continue.

Ha.

The music was still blaring and the drinks were still pouring, until suddenly the music stopped. A few seconds went by and were followed by Annette screaming.

"WHO STOLE MY FUCKING iPOD!?!" She yelled as the entire room went silent. "Nobody go anywhere! GIVE IT BACK! IT'S MY BIRTHDAY DAMNIT!"

Oh yes, this evening was full of excitement.

It became apparent as the moments of silence went by that nobody was going to give her the iPod back, so she began clearing people out. As I walked toward the door, I was invited to Garrett's house for a party.

"The party doesn't have to stop here!" his roommate said to me.

"Yeah! Come on over!" he said to me.

"Sure! I'll drive!" I said considering that I had sobered up enough to make it the block back to my apartment.

As we made our way toward the door, a sobbing Annette stopped me.

"Brittney will you PLEASE give this girl a ride home?"

"Uhh…where does she live? I am going to the Villas…like a block away," I told her, trying to get out of it.

"I live at Atwater and Park," the girl slurred at me.

"Dude…" I began looking at Annette.

"IT'S MY FUCKING BIRTHDAY!" Annette screamed at me.

And so, I was going to drive this random girl home.

Before we even got in the car, I asked her if she was going to be sick. She assured me that she was fine, and that she would not puke in my car. Then I noticed that she was missing a shoe. This should have tipped me off that this girl was a hot mess, but Annette had practically begged me to do her this favor. It wasn't too far, so I tried to suck it up.

I was not successful.

The girl was a bitch. I'm sorry. I know she was drunk, I understand that. But I was doing her a giant favor in driving to the opposite side of town, and she was not being nice about it.

"You're not a great driver. What the fuck is your problem?" she mumbled, "Its cold in here…it's hot in here. I don't like you."

What a gem.

When we got closer to her house, I asked again what street she lived on.

"Second and Bloomington!" she yelled at me.

I don't think that "Bloomington" is a street.

"Really?" I asked her.

"NO. God. I live behind Acacia fraternity. Just get me there," she slurred angrily.

We were not a block away from her house when she rolled down the window and began throwing up. We parked as she finished and spat some of it in my car. I walked around the car and stopped her.

"Do you have eight dollars here, or inside?" I asked her.

"Huh?"

"Do you have eight dollars? You owe me a car wash."

"Uh...no I don't think I have moneys..." she mumbled as she walked away.

Super.

Garrett, who had come with us on the adventure, moved from the backseat to the front, laughing hysterically at me.

"Stop that! I'm pissed!" I said, half laughing with him.

When we got back to Garrett's, his roommates and a few of their friends were flying high on testosterone and reminiscing about the fight that had happened after I had taken "Drunky McPuke Pants" home.

Apparently, while I was enjoying the glamour of having some random girl puke all over my car, some guy got vicious and pushed Annette towards the stairs, where Garrett's roommate, Vince, caught her. According to the shirtless, testosterone-filled men, they were beating that vicious guy's ass and, consequently, got blood all over themselves.

I had picked a good time to get out of the party and escape to the oasis that was the boys' house.

It was so much fun to be in a house full of guys after all of the girl drama I had experienced that weekend. It was fun to hear what they thought about girls, what they planned to do the next day, and listen to them go on and on about their one highlight of the evening – the fight.

All I have to say for what comes in the next few sentences is that I am dumb. Seriously. Well, perhaps "dumb" is a harsh word. Perhaps "naïve" is a better word for it. I THOUGHT I was there to hang out and make friends. I THOUGHT there were going to be more girls and more of a party.

I clearly need to stop having expectations in life.

Garrett, as it turned out, was into me. As in, he liked me (at least at the moment). How did I know this? He kissed me.

I KNOW, RIGHT?

I should have really seen it coming. I should not have offered to drive anyone home, I should not have gone in, and I should have just been done at the party.

Garrett was not terrible. He was not an awful guy. But he was NOT my type. The majority of our conversations had to do with drugs and drinking, two things that I wasn't all that experienced in. Sure, I have a drink now and again, but not to the extent that he did. He was the guy at the party carrying a handle of Jim Beam. He was the guy the very next day still drinking the Jim Beam. He was hard core.

Those are two words that rarely ever describe me.

When I got home that evening (ahem, at 5:30 A.M.....) I was sick of myself. It wasn't that I drank too much, it just had felt like I had cheated on someone that evening. After kissing football/boxing/hole-in-wall Donnie and Garrett, I just felt like my true love was being neglected.

Who was my true love exactly?

ME.

You laugh, but after living alone for a year and a half, I had grown to love my alone time a little too much. After dreaming of fame, of writing a book, and of recording an album (pretty big commitments and dreams, I daresay), spending even a moment on a meaningless boy was not a sufficient use of my time. If I was going to make it, if I was going to be as big as I wanted to become, I would have to ignore the lure of pointless boys and keep my eye on the prize.

In a rush of inspiration, I emailed a talent agent my demo, asking for her opinion of my music. I didn't think that I would ever hear back from her...I just thought I could get a realistic sense of what I could do in the industry from someone who worked in the business. I thought that if anything, the cost would be 1,000 dollars for her services.

Again with the naivety.

Want to know how much exactly it costs to make my dreams come true?

5K. Five grand. $5,000.

Not one. Not two. Not three. FIVE.

I could literally hear my mom and dad laughing from 230 miles away. We didn't have an extra five thousand dollars lying around. We didn't have an extra 50 dollars laying around.

The talent agent was really nice. She told me that I really could pursue my dreams. She told me that I needed to work on my writing a little, my pitch a lot, but that I had the passion and personality to make it happen.

Well, that was kind of nice to hear. Even though none of that really helped me at the time.

What I did not expect from this little experience was the explosion of confusion and concern that came from the Little house. My mom wanted me to aim for some sort of desk job in the music industry until my "big break" came along. My dad agreed with my mom, and wanted me to play more bar jobs until someone found me. They told me I hadn't paid my dues yet.

But I was sick of waiting.

It's hard, really hard, to know what you are meant to do from the time you are about 6 years old. It's even harder to think that it is possible that you cannot do it, and that you may never make it. I was stuck in both of these situations. I was sick of waiting. I was 21 and it felt like I had been waiting for 20 of those years for my chance at my dreams. I endured high school knowing that I would be out, and in Nashville, soon. Then I endured college believing that I would make it, and soon. It was becoming a reality that it was not going to be soon. It was becoming a reality that it might never happen at all.

Anxiety transformed into depression. Depression transformed into a black hole. Then my black hole of depression turned hormonal and I found myself devouring chocolates, crying at "The Hannah Montana Movie," and hating everyone. I was just going to die...right in my tiny, single apartment. That seemed logical at the time.

As always though, my best friend Michael came around. Our off again and on again friendship was set to be on. He drove to Bloomington to watch the IU vs. Purdue basketball game. He bought me a shot, I bought him a birthday shot, and then we just laughed and had fun. We hung out with Hannah, he made friends at a random party, and it was nice to have someone to bring around. He was perfect. When we got back to my apartment after a long evening of drinking, we watched a few movies, ate Oreos, and snuggled.

I didn't even know that I just needed someone to take care of me. I didn't know that all I wanted was just a few hours of someone looking after me, someone to talk to, and someone to hold onto when things got rough. He knew. He took care of me in a more intimate and romantic way than any guy I had ever even dated. He was my best friend. For that, I will eternally be grateful.

In the morning, I came out to the couch (where he was assigned to sleep) to a man who was already awake and getting ready to come wake me. After I showered and began getting ready for a Hoosierette event, he made me a sandwich and let me sip some of his Mountain Dew. By the time he left, I felt one hundred percent better. I could figure out an alternative for my career, right? I just needed a list of my needs and next actions. Ok. Here we go. I needed:

More work on the Guitar

Vocal Coaching (Pitchy! Need an ear for pitch!)

Writing and more writing criticism

Recording space? (Cost?)

Someone who wants to edit music videos

Oh, and a book publisher.

My happiness wore off a little bit at this point. I wasn't depressed again, just overwhelmed.

As I often did in times of pain, I sought Cosmopolitan, a.k.a "The Bible," for solace. Submerging my mind in ways to get the perfect bikini line, dating and sex advice, and style tips would inevitably lift my mood.

I took it as a good sign that my new favorite celeb Selena Gomez was on the cover. I took it as a better sign that the cover blurb about her read, "Secrets Behind Her Megastar Success." After reading about her life, her work ethic, and her dreams, I knew two things for certain.

With hard work and determination…I could do whatever I wanted.

Selena Gomez and I should become best friends.

The article depicted that the odds were stacked against the young Gomez, but she prevailed through it all to her super success. On top of all of that, she was only 19. She became famous years before that obviously, but here she had reached super success and she was younger than I was! If she could do it...I could at least take a leap of faith and try, right?

Thanks, Selena! Inspiration has returned!

I had been feeling weird all semester. I was tired and unmotivated. It sort of reached a breaking point where I literally could not stay out of bed and I could not keep food down. I thought it might be a virus, but my mind jumped even further. What if I had mono again? What if I let it go too long and I was in the hospital again?

I took a few days off. I tried to get better. I slept. I went to the health center, which told me I was fine. I still felt nauseous most of the time and exhausted the rest of the time. Was I just being lazy? Was it all in my head?

I firmly believe in the power of what my mom's friend calls "Oprah Days," or days where you just stay home and watch daytime television and rest up for the upcoming weeks. But even that didn't completely help. Now I was physically feeling better, but I was still emotionally stuck.

When you don't stay busy with an anxiety problem, you basically screw yourself. You trap yourself within your own thoughts and you do not let yourself out. When you are busy, you have breaks from your terrible thoughts. I figured this out in the middle of my terrible "Oprah Week," and set out on Thursday to classes and to have some fun.

Before I set out on my adventures for the day, and before I could self-cure my anxiety and exhaustion, I got a call from my dad. George Little is an amazing man. He has done everything for his family, has rarely missed a day of work to ensure our home and livelihood, and he's just really awesome. Despite the fact that my father has his feet firmly on the ground, he has always believed in my dreams.

He basically called to yell at me.

Ok. Not really.

He called to yell about the talent agent. He hated her. He thought she was dumb.

"She's dumb," he said to me, "Everyone has a different sound…what does she know about this music industry? Has she produced anyone good that you know of? No. Otherwise we could trust her. I say screw her and her 5,000 dollars and do this on your own."

And there it was.

I loved him for believing me. I loved him for helping me out of my funk. But I still worried that I was never going to make it. Everything I wrote, everything I recorded, everything I thought sounded dumb. Why was I so dumb?

Damn you to hell, anxiety!

But I headed out anyways…going to my first and last basketball game with Hannah, then going to see a midnight showing of

"The Vow," and laughing a ton. We had such an amazing time. It was a staple college moment. It was an amazing time, but even then, I knew that once I graduated I wanted something big for myself. It was a nagging thing in the back of my mind that ruined every single good moment. It was a little voice that said, "You may be having fun now…so enjoy it…because your dreams will die soon."

Ouch inner voice…ouch.

I came home from that night and tried to record.

I sounded terrible.

I tried to write…

I couldn't rhyme.

I couldn't do anything…so…

I cried.

I cried for the hard work I put in. I cried for the rough road in front of me. I cried for my lost dreams, and mostly, I cried for the fact that I was certain nothing else would make me as happy as performing would.

It was a multi-purpose cry.

I seemed to have a lot of those.

Crying is not productive. Sure, it is cleansing and at times necessary, but after it's over you need to dust yourself off and push for some productivity.

First step for me was planning a trip. I was headed to Nashville, Tennessee to see what I could make happen in the music industry, as well as the literary business. I wanted to release a book with a soundtrack someday. I wanted to travel the world, share my story, and let other women in situations like mine know that they are not alone. I began editing my story and searching for literary and talent agents. I made a list of recording labels and their addresses. I was ready to go.

I should add at this point that I really had no idea what to do...but it did feel good to actually do SOMETHING.

Here we go again with my productive streaks.

A few weeks later I was headed home to visit my family in Chicago. I was going to regroup, relax, and then I was going to come back to IU with full force. I knew I was having issues with my doubts about my book and my music career, but I hoped that a relaxing week with the family at home was what I needed to get going again. As I prepared my bags and got ready to head towards the airport (as I was flying home for the quick weekend), I checked my email and was in for a huge surprise.

Rewind: The week before my trip home, the Hoosierettes and I headed to Assembly Hall to see the women's basketball team play against the University of Illinois. The team and I had been doing things like this all semester in order to gain the respect of the Athletic Department, as well as the respect of the other athletic teams on campus. As per usual, we sat on the sidelines for the entirety of the game cheering and yelling. Usually, we pouted at halftime due to a lack of entertainment at that time; however, this game we were pissed for an entirely different reason.

The Athletic Department had invited the Ballroom Dance Club to perform.

I'll admit, they performed well...but since WHEN does ballroom dancing go with women's basketball? And since WHEN does the Athletic Department invite student-run organizations to perform at games? Wasn't that the Hoosierettes' goal all along?

Needless to say, I was in a state of pure outrage.

I walked home. I tore out my sparkling white and silver Hoosierette issued bow, I slammed down my dance bag, and I tore open my laptop. With my thick performance makeup smearing in a mix of sweat and tears, I began to form a solution.

I sent the department an email expressing my rage, and expecting no answer. I was insignificant to them...like they would ever answer me! But sending the email would make me feel better.

Fast Forward: So as I prepared to fly home that weekend to recharge, I unexpectedly got the response I had craved. Sure, it was a week after I had contacted them and sure, it was three years too late, but I had finally heard back from the Athletic Department.

"Just so you know. Since we met with you last fall, we have been putting together a plan to develop new student spirit sections at some of our non-revenue sport games (Women's Basketball and Volleyball in particular), and in general look for ways to enhance student sections, our different spirit groups, etc. affiliated with all of our sports. At some point this spring, I want the individuals putting together the plan and final recommendations for us to sit down with you again to get your

input and build on what you shared with us last fall. Their deadline for completing the plan and project is April 1 so hopefully we can meet with you sometime in the next few weeks. Also, I've asked Jonathan Benedek and Catherine Campbell, two of our full-time marketing staff, who work with various sports including Women's Basketball, Volleyball, and Men's Soccer to get in touch with you or another person from Hoosierettes about possibly scheduling some performances at some of our fall sports next year. They will begin putting together promotional calendars for different sports sometime in April when final schedules have been approved by the Big Ten. I apologize that we haven't kept you more in the loop regarding our plans related to all of this. Please know that we do very much appreciate your feedback and input as I think much of what you've shared with us previously, along with comments from other students, has helped kick-start our discussions and plans related to cheer squads, dance teams, spirit sections, etc. Also, I attend many IU sporting events in my role so I've definitely seen your group at different competitions/games this winter and it does not go unnoticed by our staff. Let me know your reaction to all of this above and whether you would still be willing to assist us as you complete your student tenure at IU. Many thanks. Take care."

And there it was.

Ok. It wasn't exactly what we had set out for, but it was a start. It was more than a start…it was a giant leap. Here, we were going to have performances. Here, we were going to have a shot. Here, they wanted MY advice and MY ideas for what to do next. I had set out to start something at a Big 10 university, I had overcome so many obstacles and made so many friends and enemies...and finally, here it was. My dream for this team, and for this school, was finally coming true.

So, while flying home that weekend and sitting in the airport and on the plane, I couldn't help but think, "I have accomplished one big dream...who's to say I can't do it again?"

And the inspiration continues.

Again.

That is, in fact, exactly how I pitched it to my mom. I told her that I made my dream of the dance team happen, despite the odds and the difficulties. Didn't she have faith that I could publish my book and begin my singing career?

"Honey," she said, "I just don't want to set you up for disappointment."

But I knew I wouldn't be too distressed. It took 3.5 years for me to get someone in the Athletic Department to notice my team...I had learned to be patient and deal with disappointment. I could do this, I assured her.

For all I know she still hasn't bought it...

When I headed into Midway Airport in Chicago to go back to Indianapolis, my head was in the clouds. I was thinking hard about how my life could soon be full of airports and security, of singing and signing, of stress, but of my dreams. Life was so good.

Until he smacked me.

He didn't mean to, but the TSA agent directing the lines at security just hit me in the face as he was directing people.

It could have been my fault since I wasn't paying much attention. It didn't hurt...but it was sort of like someone out there was determined to bring me down out of the clouds. The smack brought me back to earth and reminded me that the present is here, waiting to be lived. "Stop daydreaming!" was what that smack told me. To apologize, the TSA agent pushed me to the front of the line so I wouldn't have to wait. "Ah, the Gods are smiling on me again," I thought.

False.

I was pulled to the side for a random test and ion screening on my luggage. That took about ten minutes.

Sometimes, at moments like these, I am so convinced that these kinds of things happen to me and me alone.

Slightly deflated, but back down to earth, I hopped on the plane.

Then I examined my week's upcoming schedule and continued to deflate.

I had three sorority workout classes scheduled, two lengthened Hoosierette practices ahead of me, and a trip to Louisville to perform with the Hoosierettes in the upcoming week? Sounded like a fun week to stock up on Pepsi and extra sleep!

So how does a champion like me begin her busy week? By wearing her Kilroy's Bar t-shirt and sweats to bed, oversleeping for her Monday exam, rushing to the exam in the aforementioned pajamas with eyeliner smeared all over her face, and questioning whether or not she had deodorant on throughout the duration of the exam.

I am such a winner.

But the week itself was kicked off (although not well...), and I knew it needed to be a productive one. I had nine weeks left until graduation. Those nine weeks needed to be smooth, fun, but, most of all, useful. I needed to set myself a strong foundation to kick off into my post-education chapter of my life.

It's the final countdown, ladies and gentlemen. In the spirit of setting a "strong foundation" to my "post-education" future, I began to look into music experiences, as well as writing exhibition opportunities. I had been hearing about a competition called "Campus Superstar" through my teammates for a while. Basically, it was Indiana's version of American Idol for college students. The grand prize was 5,000 dollars and I am not going to lie: I ~~wanted~~ needed the money.

When the morning of the auditions happened, I really didn't want to go. I know I am not the best singer in the world. In fact, a talent agent herself had just told me that. My teammates Taylor and Annette urged me to go, "Just try it! What do you have to lose?"

I used to be such a sucker for peer pressure.

So, three hours late and without practice, I drove over to the auditions.

I clomped up the stairs of the building in my caramel colored leather boots (God, I loved those shoes...) tossed my hair over one shoulder, and opened the door.

The second I walked in the door, I knew I was out of my league. I tried to keep my confidence, but let's face it: confidence is NOT my middle name.

When I walked into the actual audition room (after a nerve wracking wait), I walked over to the table with the judges. There sat a few professional types, a few artsy types, and an IU celebrity: Daniel W.

Daniel produced and co-wrote the IU basketball anthem "This is Indiana," as well as a few other Indiana University classics. As far as campus superstars went, he was THE one. I was temporarily star-struck.

I shook each judge's hand and introduced myself...they seemed perplexed.

"Well that doesn't happen often..." I heard one murmur.

Oops?

I joked with each of them, they laughed a lot, and they told me that I had amazing energy. I figured that this was a great way to start out the audition. Then came the main event: the music. In my personal opinion, I sang my little heart out and sounded great.

Raise your hand if you think I am going to actually succeed at something for once in my college career!

Ha ha. Fooled you.

I never got called back.

I know that the saying goes that "if God closes a door he opens a window," but at some point can't God bring in a bulldozer and knock the whole building down so I can go wherever I want? Is that too much to ask?

Yeah...I wasn't bitter or anything.

I wouldn't even hold on to the anger. I would let it go. Right?

WRONG.

I wasn't mad that I was not chosen. I know that rejection was a part of life. My issue is that the thing I wanted to do with the rest of my life did not come naturally to me. I really just was not that good at it. My bad mood really started there, but it was not being contained very well.

For example, my conversations were going a little something like this:

Hannah: "Hey!!"

Me: "HI. I am in a record-breaking shitty mood. Did you know our Athletic Department spent 1 million dollars on a new training center? OH GOOD! I WAS FUCKING WORRIED THAT OUR FOOTBALL TEAM WOULD GO WITHOUT A STATE OF THE ART TREADMILL!"

Hannah: "I like it when you're mad at the world."

Well, that made one of us.

My exploding anger carried over into my academics. What was the point anymore? Who cared about literature and statistics? I was getting a degree in something I didn't care about, to go on to do things I didn't care about, and then die.

Drama Queen, party of one.

How many times in college would I need a major attitude readjustment?

Eight weeks left. Just eight more weeks.

If I didn't die first.

Later that week, I was taking a shower (as I generally try to) and, suddenly, I saw a great flash of light. Then I heard a huge crash. Now, being naked and wet and all, I was pretty sure death was upon me. Fearing for my life, I snuck my head around the shower curtain.

The light fixture had fallen out of the ceiling. Now that could *not* be safe.

I swear these things only happen to me.

My supreme anxiety issues would have made it easy to sink into another hole of despair. I could just cry and whine and write and do all the usual things I did when little things pissed me off...but at this point I had had enough.

I was just plain mad, and I was going to come back fighting.

I spent the past three and a half years fearing myself and the situations I got myself into. I spent three and a half years getting easily discouraged...and why was that? I had endured a very rough college experience and I was on the road to graduate, I had written (most of) a book, I had written hundreds of songs, I had created a dance team...I had even gotten a brown belt in tae kwon do since I had gotten to college. Yes, I had hit a ton of obstacles...but I had overcome all of them. This "Campus Superstar" thing was just a flicker on my radar. Why let it bother me? Why not make some noise in my last few weeks as a co-ed?

I love these inspirational moments. So I was back to the girl who was out to change the world, yet again.

And this time, it was going to last.

Ha. For your sake, I hope it does too. This everlasting roller coaster of drama and fear could go on for a few thousand more pages.

It's probably obvious by now that I love new starts. I don't like endings, but I love beginnings. So, it makes sense that when it comes to vacations I absolutely love packing. I make tons of lists, I pack way in advance, and I coordinate outfits with a crazy amount of shoes. To me road trips, flights, and walks...they're all worth packing for. On my maiden voyage to Nashville to research the probability of a music career, I was packed for two solid weeks before departure. Should I bring my suit for interviews? My boots for a night on the town? I didn't know so...I packed it all! I knew my chances of getting my "big break" in the three days I would be there were low...but I got excited anyways. To me, Nashville was the place that held my dreams. Nashville was a place where anything could happen. Nashville was as close to heaven as a girl like me could get, and if Nashville was heaven, Toby Keith was my God.

I wanted NOTHING more than to meet him. He was a guy that could understand me. He was, in a word, a badass in the country world and besides a never-ending list of female singers and songwriters; he was at the top of my list of people to meet. I was obsessed with the concept that one day he would meet me, hear me, and want to sign me to his label.

Well...a girl can dream, can't she?

Don't normal girls dream of having some celebrity as their boyfriend? Or of being in the next Twilight movie or Hunger Games film? While all of those things sounded great...I had my eye on a different prize.

"Taylor Swift sang a song
About her love for a man and a Tim McGraw Song
Made it big on the radio...
Now I'm not tryin to be like her
But I've got a country man I'm dyin to sing for
More like, a guy I wana be

(Chorus)
I wana a be a badass like Toby Keith
I wana sing for the troops and grit my teeth
In the desert, the country, everywhere in between
I wana bend them strings and sing sing sing
I wana drink out of that Red Cup and see the US
One nation under God
I wana raise my glass, kick some ass and be
As cool as Toby

Now I know I'm the type of girl
Who should sing about boys and peace in the world
But that never was my cup of tea
Wana wear a bandana down in the south
Never wana be a "lady" and shut my mouth
I'm here to let freedom ring!

(Chorus)
I wana a be a badass like Toby Keith
I wana sing for the troops and grit my teeth
In the desert, the country, everywhere in between
I wana bend them strings and sing sing sing
I'll ask "How do you like me now?" and talk about me
One nation under God
I wana raise my glass, kick some ass and be
As cool as Toby

I'm an American girl, through and through
I love this country, and its music too.
Country girls have all the class

> *There are many singers in this industry*
> *Ones who stand up for their beliefs*
> *But very few are this badass*
>
> *(Chorus)*
> *I wana a be a badass like Toby Keith*
> *I wana sing for the troops and grit my teeth*
> *In the desert, the country, everywhere in between*
> *I wana bend them strings and sing sing sing*
> *I wana live in that Trailerhood and smoke with Willy*
> *One nation under God*
> *I raise my glass, kick some ass and be*
> *As cool as Toby"*

No sense in me wasting time pretending to be ashamed of the fact I wrote a song about him, because I am not. Sure, it is dorky. Sure, it is desperate. But I believed that the magic of this melody would lure in a record deal for me.

So, over-packed suitcase in hand and a songbook in my purse, I set out to Nashville.

TO MEET TOBY.

Spoiler Alert: I never met Toby.

Kathy and I left at 7:15 A.M. That's right: I went on spring break with my mom. No sense in pretending to be ashamed of that either. I love hanging out with my mom. Our flight had maybe fifty people on it, leaving us with plenty of space and lots of extra pretzels and peanuts. I took this as my first good sign.

When we got to Nashville, a book I was currently reading that I had gotten many years ago was on display in the airport. It was everywhere. In stores, on display outside of a café…it was strange. Because it was not newly released, this struck me as odd. Perhaps it was fate? Perhaps it was God telling me I was on the right path?

Or perhaps it was a coincidence.

I chose exactly what I wanted it to be: fate.

When we got our rental car (a beautiful Jeep Wrangler), we headed out of the airport. My mom and I were, in a word, clueless. We had no idea where we were heading, what we were doing, or how to work the car. A friend of mine, and my former youth minister, Christine was very helpful in giving me a list of things to accomplish before we left on the trip. But other than Christine's half sheet of paper (saying things like "meet Toby Keith," "Hard Rock Café" and "find job opportunities"), we had no definite plans.

I took it personally, however, when the radio played a song I particularly loved or when the girl at the airport liked my one shouldered floral top…I was convinced that I was going to get discovered and that I was on the right track.

I selectively notice these kinds of things.

Our first stop on the adventure was the historic Ryman Auditorium, the original location of the Grand Ole Opry, or the big Kahuna, in my opinion. In starting our backstage tour with Art, our 80 year old tour guide, I looked around when he asked where we were from. Half the people in the tour were from Mississippi, some from California, and some from scattered southern states. With my mom and me the only Chicagoans there, I figured that everyone else was a bigger, more die hard country music fan than we were. Oddly enough, I was wrong.

We kicked their asses in country trivia.

When I was at a party in my sophomore year of college, a boy from southern Indiana told me that I was not a legitimate country fan because I was from the north. He told me that I knew nothing about country, because as much as I tried and as much as I called myself a cowgirl, I would never truly know much about country music being from 'way up north.'

I now say to that jackass: HA.

When Art asked what duet Johnny Cash and his wife June Carter were singing in a particular picture, the answer came to me immediately though I did not shout it out. When he looked at the group from Jackson, Mississippi and asked them what song it was, they didn't know.

"It's where you're from…" I whispered to the family to help them answer his question.

"Where I am from?" The woman guessed.

"Jackson!" I nearly screamed.

Geez.

Then when the tour guide talked about Dolly Parton and her parting song to her TV show co-host, I nearly dropped dead in awe when everyone in the room thought Whitney Houston (may she rest in peace) wrote "I Will Always Love You."

Why tour the Ryman if you know nothing about country?

When we finally were at the end of our tour, the guides let you take pictures on the historic stage. It was a chilling feeling being onstage where so many legendary performers have stood. This was what I wanted. More than anything else in the world, this was what it was all about for me.

The woman I helped out in the quizzing portion of the evening stood in the audience.

"Sing something," she said.

"Huh?" I asked unintelligently.

"How cool would it be to say you sang on stage at the Ryman auditorium?" she replied.

So I sang.

It was possibly one of the greatest moments of my life. Yet another one of those moments that I knew, I just KNEW that this was exactly where I was supposed to be.

So close, and yet so far.

After our tour of the Ryman, we went to explore the areas around our hotel. We were placed right near my personal hot spot, Music Row. We drove on over there to see what it was all about. In my first five minutes on Music Row, however, we were going the wrong direction.

No, seriously. My mother had us heading the wrong way on a one way street.

Five minutes on Music Row and I was heading to my certain death. AWESOME.

We eventually got turned around and back to our hotel with a few screams, several U-turns, and getting yelled at by a few Tennessee drivers (sorry Nashville!). Up until that point, I felt like my trip was a godsend. Even going wrong on Music Row, I was certain that this would be the best trip ever.

My enthusiasm died slightly when we saw the hotel room.

"It's ok that the room is crap," I coached myself, "We are still in Nashville and we are still going to the Opry tonight. Focus on that."

So we prepared ourselves and got ready for our drive.

As we stepped out into the sweet Tennessee air, I had a moment to smile to myself. My mom was dressed in a deep red and black top, black jeans, and her black cherry boots. I wore a black and silver cheetah print dress and my black cowboy boots.

We looked hot.

In the time that I was sitting in the Grand Ole Opry House, I had another moment of immense adoration. I wanted nothing more than to perform there, to sing there where so many legends have sang before.

One might think, at this point, that it would become depressing having all of these thoughts. After all, there are like a billion people in the U.S. and only like one hundred become country music singers. After that there are only like fifty of them that maintain a career after their first radio single. What would make me feel like I was any different than the thousands of others that want that same sort of fame?

Nah. It wasn't depressing at all.

The next morning we headed back to Music Row. I was determined to hand out my demos and to see what kind of feedback I could get in Music City.

At one of the bigger record companies, they told me they did not take unsolicited materials. At another, I was directed to join a songwriter's guild. At yet another, I was encouraged to achieve success in something else in order to get the contacts needed to have a songwriting career. It should have been devastating, hearing that the chances of me having success in the music business were slim to none, but it really wasn't. Everyone I talked to was really encouraging and supportive. I gained a lot of information, but also, more importantly, motivation. After a quick nap, we headed out to shop and bar hop. Not many girls can say that they like spending time with their mothers...but I can. We had a lot of fun eating barbeque and drinking margaritas. It seemed like a shame that we would have to leave the next day.

On our last day in Nashville, it rained. Actually, that word is not accurate enough to describe what happened. Torrential downpour does not even describe this weather. It was more like taking a zillion shower heads and placing them over the city on high blast. Add some lightning and thunder and you have the day.

We opted out of walking around town that day (again...did I mention the weather?) and went to the mall.

UNFORTUNATELY, due to the great floods of 2010, there was only one store and the movie theater open in the mall.

Crap.

So my mother and I spent half the day in the Opryland Hotel being jealous of our surroundings and the rest of the day at the movie theater and the one store that was open.

Then, our flight was delayed due to the weather.

The optimistic version of me would have looked at the flight delay as God's way of keeping me in Nashville until I landed my big break.

The other part of me (which at the time was a good 95 percent of me) just wanted to go home.

We eventually made it home and I wasn't sad to see Nashville go. I knew I would be back, and soon.

I had a blessed three day return to Chicago to visit with my dad, spend even more time with my mom, become acquainted with my brother's best friend from the Navy, Jay, and reacquainted with my own brother, Johnny. When I headed back that Sunday it hit me again: I was a senior. This could be one of the last times I would drive back to school from a break. This was it. Time was about to start passing very quickly.

The five hours I spent in traffic were not quick.

The ten minutes I spent at a bar trying to visit Michael did not go fast enough.

The subsequent argument Michael and I had after I ditched his ass did not blow over quickly enough.

The week leading up to the biggest Hoosierette performance of the year did not pass me by with any kind of ease.

When will I understand? Life is never what I expect it to be.

Six more weeks. Just six more weeks...

In my last six weeks of being the Hoosierettes' dance team captain, I had planned on enjoying myself. I had planned on kicking butt at the Indianapolis Pacers performance, wowing the Athletic Department with our skill and dedication, and exciting the crowds at the Relay for Life and Little 500 performances we had coming up. My plans were big, and the dedication I was to have to it was going to have to be bigger.

In the week back from spring break, I had my second (Or was it third? Maybe fourth?) meeting with the Athletic Department. This time, instead of meeting with older guys with kids and retirement funds, I met with a student intern.

He was so attractive I could barely pay attention.

Then, it came to my attention that our biggest performance, a pre-game dance at an Indianapolis Pacers game, had begun to fall apart. The online ticket server had crashed, losing a good amount of the tickets we had ordered. Then the coordinator would not get back to me about this issue, our transportation questions, and more. I received emails, phone calls, and Facebook messages from parents and dancers about this issue daily.

This was one of the parts I didn't like about being the team captain. I like when people are nice. I like when things are going well. Who doesn't? But when things don't go my way...I tend to try and ignore it. I am just one of those people. Not Hannah. Hannah jumps in with two feet to get what she needs. Hannah is not easily diffused. I needed a little bit of Hannah in me to talk to the Pacers.

Three phone calls, forty-five minutes of total phone time, and three emails to my team. That is what it took to be like Hannah.

That's a lot of effort, if you ask me.

If I had a hard time calling a basketball team about a few lost tickets, I was not yet cut out for the real world.

Suddenly those six weeks before graduation were necessary to my growth and maturity.

Later on in the "practice process for the Pacers performance," I noticed that one of the dancers on our team simply did not know the moves for the performance. After spending three full months on it, the girl could not remember most of the dance. As a captain, I had to make a decision. On a personal level, I loved the girl. On a personal level, I did not want to discourage a single person on the team. On a professional level, she was not doing the work that the rest of the team was doing to ensure a great performance. On a professional level…she sucked.

Here we were: the Hoosierettes had me facing another real world issue. I had to do what was professional. I emailed her a warning and asked her to practice, but if the dance was not good enough in the coming week, she was out of the dance.

UGH.

I honestly thought that she would email me back and say something like "Screw you!" or "Who do you think you are?" I lived in fear of opening my email, in case a particularly rude message was heading my way. Instead though, she showed up to practice looking confident and practiced in the dance.

#winning.

The week of the Pacers performance went a little something like this:

Monday: Practice. We rocked it. This lulled me into a false sense of excitement and confidence.

Tuesday: The Pacers people sent all of the tickets to the wrong addresses. I freaked out.

Wednesday: We practiced again. I suck at pretty much everything. Then I cried.

Thursday: The BIG DAY.

Ok. So we didn't perform in front of the thousands of fans that I thought we were going to (as it happens, the Indiana Pacers were not, in fact, a premiere NBA team at the time), but we did get to perform in front of our family and friends, as they got to see what we had worked on for the past three months. As I took center court, I could not stop beaming. I had done it. This was a dream come true.

We danced our hearts out.

Sitting in the front row were the parents of each Hoosierette, including my own, my brother, and his best friend. It meant the world to me that they were there. Only my parents would drive three hours for a two minute performance.

My biggest collegiate dream had been accomplished. I had gotten the Hoosierettes on the map with an NBA game performance. On to my next dream: spending every day of my life doing what I loved.

If only my plan were less vague...

As only a true future author and forever book enthusiast would, somewhere in my senior year I read the Hunger Games series. When I say "I read them" I really mean "I devoured them." Within the span of four days, I had read all three books. I was enthralled. I like to say that, "I grew up with Harry, went to college with Bella, and graduated with Katniss." No matter how much people call these series "phenomena" or "fad books," they mark a generation. So, as a true member of that generation, I went to the midnight viewing of the Hunger Games, starring Jennifer Lawrence.

In preparation for the movie, my mom bought me a *Glamour* magazine, as well as *Seventeen*, with Jennifer on the cover. She said that her brothers urged her parents to encourage her acting, saying that it was her "sport." She joked that she was a pretty good student, but when she read a script she really felt like that's where she shined.

After watching her shine in the movie, those words stuck in my mind. Did I feel like I shined when I sang? A little. Did I shine when I wrote? A little. But where did I shine the most?

It's always about me! Aren't I such a conceited bitch sometimes?

Don't answer that.

I loved reading these success stories. I loved seeing magazines full of stars that had worked hard and paid their dues to get where they were. The problem with my particular dream, however, was that it all depended on the approval of an ambiguous "they." My dreams do not depend on the potential readers of my book, the potential listeners of my music, or any other fan of my creativity. No, my dreams depend on a boardroom of stuffy executives who barely know me. My dreams depend on a bunch of people with degrees in judgment. Without passing the tests of these people, my dreams could not even begin to come true.

Needless to say, I didn't like that idea.

What do a bunch of people in boardrooms know about us? So they have statistics and theories...that can mean nothing! Sometimes the greatest things lay outside statistical analysis.

I'll admit. It was a cocky thought and a gamble. But since when was I rational when it came to achieving my dreams? I needed to start achieving. I needed a plan. I would self publish first. I would make my records on my computer and sell them were I could. I didn't need these people's approval. I just needed my dreams to come true.

And if I so happened to befriend Selena Gomez, Toby Keith, and Jennifer Lawrence along the way, so be it.

Meanwhile, as I decided how I would proceed to follow my dreams, I did need to attend to real life matters. As my final weeks went on, my Hoosierette captainship was rapidly ending. My heart was incredibly torn. I wanted to remain on the team for forever, and to continue work on the group...but it was also time to let them grow on their own. Our very last performance was to be at Little 500. We would dance in front of the gates as students went in. Because all year long the girls wanted to do a hip-hop routine, I finally relented. We would have hip hop auditions. If you made it, you would perform that one dance. If not...no big deal. The girls did not initially try out for a hip hop team, and I thought that this would be a fair way to make cuts so we would have a small group of girls for the routine.

Sound sensible so far?

We had try outs for the one dance. We made cuts. Then, the "Twitter Scandal Sequel" began.

The girl who was initially angered by the Original Twitter Scandal, Korin, did not make the hip hop routine. Everyone else who did not make it had no problems. Korin, however, was livid. It started out vague, with tweets about her general rage and disappointment in life. Then she called the routine and other things a joke.

Needless to say…we were all in a tizzy.

When Katherine and Michelle, the two girls who were about to inherit my captainship, asked me what I was going to do about it…I initially freaked out. This was the part of the job I hated. This was the part of the experience that I did not enjoy. But with two weeks left until I graduated…why did I have to deal with it?

Senior Year Rule Number 12: Quit while you're ahead.

"So, Brittney?" Katherine asked, "What are you going to do?"

My final answer? "Nothing."

I was done with the drama. Sick of having to be the bad guy. Michelle and Katherine were about to be co-captains so they could practice their captain skills. THEY could deal with this.

And they did.

Reading the emails they sent out was heartwarming. They knew professionalism, they knew how to be authoritative, and they did a great job. After watching them deal with the situation, I knew they could handle the team next year.

Unfortunately, with several emails sent, Korin did not apologize. She showed up to practice that night as if nothing happened.

Crap. Now I had to step in.

We stepped out into the hallway to talk and I was struck with such a strange feeling. First of all, I was in no way uncomfortable with dealing with a teammate that had disrespected us. I kept a calm head and spoke with her with the maturity she deserved...something I could not have handled years ago. Second of all, I really had assembled an amazing group of girls. Korin and I had a semi-rational conversation and came to a simple agreement. Then, she stood in front of our entire team and apologized to them. It says so much about the character of our team that she could do that. It said so much about the character of our teammates that they erupted in applause after she spoke. It was like being a mother watching her children make a big step. I was just so proud of each of them.

So we headed into Little 500. My senior Little 500. I could not handle my excitement. I threw my "no expectations means no disappointments" mantra out the window. I was ready for an amazing week.

The most amazing night of Little 500 that year had nothing to do with the race. It had nothing to do with the endless drinking and partying. It had everything to do with one sober Wednesday night. For the first time ever, the Hoosierettes were going to have an awards night.

The Saturday before awards night, I spent nine hours making awards for the girls. I attached photos of the team to construction paper, decorated with stickers, and even wrote out personal notes to each and every one of them, thanking them for a good season. I found that I had an inside joke with or at least a small attachment to each girl, which really says a lot about a leader. I had connected with each of my eighteen dancers, something that not every team captain could do. When it came time for awards night, I beamed with pride at the girls as I gave them the credit which they so much deserved.

What I did not anticipate was winning team MVP.

What I also did not anticipate was it turning into "senior night."

Senior Year Rule Number 13: Be humble.

I never did any of this for credit. I did this because I wanted to, and eventually because it was what I loved. Having all eighteen of my team members make me a scrapbook full of memories came as a huge shock to me. Having my team members present me with gifts that they had made me was a huge shock to me. I looked around a room with each of these girls and was overcome with emotion. This was what I set out to do. We had worked so hard, we had accomplished so much, but my own personal road with the Hoosierettes was over.

Ouch.

This team had defined my four years of college. It was my purpose for the four years I was there. I know school was supposed to be my purpose, and normal people find peace with that or with that and a bottle of booze. Not me. This was what I wanted to accomplish. What was going to become my purpose after senior night, when I handed off the captainship?

Crap.

Upcoming graduation seemed to overshadow everything at that point. It was not about my senior Little 500 anymore. It was not about the fun "end of the year" parties that happen in such a college town. It was about the light at the end of the tunnel, and simply getting there in one piece.

Because of my insane mindset I nearly forgot about my 22nd birthday.

I did not end up in the hospital like I did a few days after my 21st. Instead, I had an amazing and stress-free day. I went and saw an early movie, ate a ton of food, and then drank with my best friends. For one day, and one day only, the fear of graduation was suspended.

After my 22nd birthday, however, it really started to wear on me. Graduation without a job prospect in sight was setting off the panic button in my mind and a set of mood swings that was impossible to escape. I had come to college with the knowledge that the things I wanted to do with the rest of my life could not be attained with a degree, but I was told that without an education I would never get a job. However…with this education I was not getting a job either, which was incredibly frustrating. Four years, thousands of dollars, countless hours studying and panicking, and I was no closer to my dreams at all. All I had was a book of my funny collegiate escapades, a binder full of songs, and a dream.

Hello, panic attack.

It was all I could do to keep this panic and frustration from my parents. They had worked so hard to get me to where I was…I couldn't bear to upset them with my worries that it was all for nothing. So I spent my nights wrapped in an old Army t-shirt and my underwear and curled up on a bed of memories. I looked at every aspect of my college career…from "The Detroit Incident" to the "David Era" to the near-death experiences I had in both my sophomore and junior years, and I tried to make sense of it all. Maybe, just maybe, I could draw a line. Maybe I could find the meaning in it all, and the anxieties about leaving would let up a little bit.

Can't say I didn't try!

Here's a little known tidbit about graduation week: nothing of consequence gets accomplished. You are literally biding time, and occasionally packing. Do you have a job lined up? If no, sleep is out of the question. You are too busy filling out applications. Ha. You say you are leaving for an internship the day after graduation? Enjoy having tape and boxes everywhere as you pack frantically.

Graduation, it seems, is not as glamorous as one might think.

The night before graduation, I did not sleep at all. Literally. We were staying at a lake house in the middle of the woods and not only was I anxious and excited, but I was having the biggest allergy attack ever. Around 5:30 A.M., my friend Brett texted me and told me that since I couldn't sleep, I should go upstairs, watch the sun rise and grab a cup of coffee (I replaced "coffee" with "Pepsi" and we had a deal). So I did just that. He also told me to revel in the excitement and the moment of the day. I looked back on the four years with a smile and looked forward to the future. I sank into the peace and quiet of my alone time, but was thankful for the company of my dad. It was nice to get alone time with both of my parents before the big day. It calmed me. It focused me. It readied me for what was to come.

Before the ceremony Hannah, Lizzie, and my cousin Alyssa started a new tradition. We poured a shot and shouted "Cheers!" to the graduates. Everyone who was closest to me was going to be there. It was perfect. I knew, surrounded by these people, that I could do anything. Job or no job, I was ready.

And then…it happened. I graduated.

Epilogue:

And there he was...a perfect man. Right there at my graduation ceremony. He looked like Zac Efron, with piercing blue eyes and giant biceps and we instantly fell in love. Then, out of all the students on campus, I was voted to be the student commencement speaker. As I looked out into the crowd, I smiled knowing that we all made it. We all survived. I was so proud. The second I stepped off the stage, a man approached me and offered me a record deal. I looked up into the sky and saw pigs flying...how funny.

Ok. So that's not what happened.

Epilogue 2: What REALLY Happened

It really ended with long hair. I had grown it out for almost two years, and was determined to have it perfect for graduation pictures. With all of my friends and family in the audience (and okay, a bloodstream half full of liquor), I stood with my class as we received the recognition we deserved. The worst four years I had ever loved were over. I fought hangovers, mean boyfriends, broken hearts, health issues, and so much more just to get to this point – and yet, it had gone by so fast.

I had my final moment of pure awe in college that day. As if time had stopped, I got to look around with my fellow graduates and remember how much we had all been through. Only four years ago, we had been inducted into the university, and now we were being inducted into the real world. For a moment, I was nostalgic and wished that it could continue.

Only for a moment.

It was a bittersweet ending to the toughest journey I had ever been on, but I knew after surviving this I could do anything.

I was on my way, and I couldn't wait.

Question: Am I allowed to have a Post-Epilogue Epilogue?

Answer: I DO WHAT I WANT

Family: After graduation I moved back in with my mom and dad, who were as cool as possible about the whole thing. They really supported me through the whole "finding myself" phase of post-graduation and into the job application process. Without them, I could not have gone to, nor survived, college. Even my brother was an amazing help. If anything, this crazy experience brought me even closer to them.

Boys: I never found "the one" in college. A lot of girls go to college for that reason...but honestly, it just doesn't always work that way. My cousin Emma would hate that I am saying this, but those kinds of things happen in their own time. Unfortunately, you cannot push it and I am okay with that. Michael and I are still friends, but at a great distance. We just don't connect like we used to. I never said goodbye to Jacob, something I regret because he taught me so many difficult college lessons. I have spoken to neither David nor Cole since college has ended, and I am totally okay with that. They served their purpose in my life, I thank them for that, but I am in no way interested in rekindling a friendship with them. Fool me once...

Lizzie: Lizzie and I found bliss once I moved back home. She was my rock through grad weekend and kept my feet on the ground and my emotions in check. Without her, who knows where I would be? Our relationship is proof that true friendship can make it through anything.

Hannah: I never realized how much two people can teach one another until I met her. Through college, she taught me how to stand up for myself, while I taught her patience (because let's face it: you need a lot of patience to deal with me). I think distance will be tough on us in the coming years, but I know ours is a friendship that will last forever. Hannah is now currently a Mary Kay consultant, an advocate for children in courts in Indiana, and working in just so many different capacities to change the world.

Me: Where am I now? For starters, I am still praying for my fame and success. I still want to sing, I continue to write, and I am basically waiting for my miracle. I pray for this book to drive someone, somewhere to finish college or persevere in whatever they do. I know this story is not hugely inspiring, nor is the ending amazing (I do not become a vampire, I do not vanquish a dark wizard, nor do I fight 23 other people to death, thus changing the world in some way), but it's real. Everything that I have written is about my college experience. Names have been changed protect the (not so) innocent (and to keep my house from being egged), but it all happened. If I can survive university life, anyone, anywhere can.

Acknowledgements:

I would of course like to thank my parents for telling me that I could essentially do this and do well at it. Without them, none of this would be possible and I owe them for eternity. Thank you to my brother for being so supportive in college... I would have no car, and no sanity without him! I would also like to thank each of the characters in this saga. Most importantly I'd like to thank my friends "Hannah" and "Lizzie," without whom I would not have survived college –nor would this book be nearly as good. I'd like to mention my friend Hope who literally gave me "hope" through my college experience and Lauren who won't mind that this acknowledgement is not as witty as Hope's and love me anyways. Thanks to my tallest friend Natalie, for the editing and encouragement. Without your enthusiasm and late night discussions, I would have never made it out of IU alive. Thanks to my cousin Katie for reading this, editing this, and commenting on all aspects of this before I sent it out! Couldn't have done it without you, your grammatical expertise and your legal advice! A special thanks goes out to every Hoosierette (past, present, and future) for keeping up the tradition I began. Without that team and this story, my college experience would be obsolete. Thanks also to D-Bill, Mike Brennan, and Christine Collins for being second parents to me and encouraging this crazy dream as well. To my oldest friend Katie, thank you for all the fun summers and crazy soundtracks that became the background music to my life in those four years. To my Aunt Bev and Uncle Fred, I am nothing at all without your help, support, and the lazy summer days spent at the pool with you guys. Thank you! Finally, thanks to Tayler, Kristen, and Danielle, my dance team buddies. They, in addition to everyone previously listed, encouraged me to put the pen to the paper and get this story written. Without all of the days

Tayler and I spent casting the people we would put in this movie, without all of the talking and editing, I would not have been nearly as inspired to do this. Thank you all for your continued support! I love you all!

For more information on the crazy adventures of Brittney Little like the book on Facebook at www.facebook.com/makesagoodstory , follow it at @makesagoodstory on Twitter, and visit www.youtube.com/brittannlittle.

www.ingramcontent.com/pod-product-compliance
Lightning Source LLC
Chambersburg PA
CBHW070557100426
42744CB00006B/319